VIVA
COLDPLAY!
A BIOGRAPHY

VIVA
COLDPLAY!
A BIOGRAPHY
MARTIN ROACH

OMNIBUS PRESS

London / New York / Paris / Sydney / Copenhagen / Berlin / Madrid / Tokyo

Copyright © 2010 Omnibus Press
(A Division of Music Sales Limited)

Cover designed by Fresh Lemon
Picture research by Jacqui Black

ISBN: 978.1.84938.546.6
Order No: OP53647

The Author hereby asserts his/her right to be identified as the author of this work in accordance with Sections 77 to 78 of the Copyright, Designs and Patents Act 1988.

Exclusive Distributors
Music Sales Limited,
14/15 Berners Street,
London, W1T 3LJ.

Music Sales Corporation,
257 Park Avenue South,
New York, NY 10010, USA.

Macmillan Distribution Services,
56 Parkwest Drive
Derrimut, Vic 3030,
Australia.

Every effort has been made to trace the copyright holders of the photographs in this book but one or two were unreachable. We would be grateful if the photographers concerned would contact us.

Typeset by: Phoenix Photosetting, Chatham, Kent
Printed in the EU

You can visit the Make Trade Fair website for more information at: www.maketradefair.com

A catalogue record for this book is available from the British Library.

Visit Omnibus Press on the web at www.omnibuspress.com

Contents

Author's Acknowledgements

The author wishes to acknowledge and thank the following magazines, radio stations and websites for their extensive coverage of Coldplay's career to date:

Amazon.com	NME & NME.com
A Beautiful World	The Observer
BeQueen.de	OK!
The Brain Farm Magazine	Online.ie
The Cleveland Plain Dealer	Q
Contactmusic.com	Rolling Stone
Details	Select
Entertainment Weekly	ShakeStir
Esquire	Sleeveage.com
Flavour.Lookon.net	Spin
The Guardian	The Sun
Heat	tagesanzeiger.ch
The Independent	Timesleader.com
Melody Maker	VH1
Mojo	Virgin Radio
MTV News	W Magazine
Music Week	X Ray

Special thanks to Simon Williams and all at Fierce Panda, and Chris Allison at Sonic360.com.

Introduction

Among the more fascinating aspects of the music industry is its ability to produce the unpredictable. In an almost cyclical process of tedious negativity, generational naysayers have made a career bemoaning the death of originality and invention in music, tired as they are of an endless tide of pop wannabes. Their rancour has never been more apparent than in the 'reality TV' age of overnight music sensations. Yet for all these complaints, for all the lightweight pop stars, for all the predictable re-issues by dinosaur rock acts, periodically a band comes along that writes their own script. An act that doesn't necessarily win favour among the corners of the critics' lounge, but ploughs their own furrow regardless. Coldplay is just such a band.

Initially described as "the new U2/Travis/Radiohead" et al, or "knobhead students/bedwetters", Coldplay in their early days had the ability to frustrate and delight in equal measure. However, as they released album after album of superlative music, backed up by relentless touring schedules that put most other large bands to shame, the tide turned. The critics' barbed pens were softened; the musical snobs fell silent. Coldplay's recorded output has justifiably enjoyed critical plaudits that few bands could dream of, quickly matched by mammoth commercial success. Yet their moral stance on numerous issues has attracted its fair share of largely undue criticism – as indeed has their quiet approach to life as a modern rock band.

The centre of Coldplay's world is undoubtedly Chris Martin, its lead singer and visual presence. Despite his avowed revulsion to the cult of celebrity, in a few short years his band's meteoric success thrust him unwittingly into an intense media spotlight, bringing with it an inevitable flurry of rumour and gossip. His apparent fragility and lack of confidence might seem to contradict his acclaimed musical talent, but this same insecurity is the very fuel to Coldplay's fire. Without this, the band would probably not exist, at least not in the form that we know.

How they came from nowhere to become one of the world's biggest bands is a story centred mostly around their stunning catalogue of music, but also one that takes in Hollywood actresses, internal disputes, frequent uncertainty about the future and high-profile music biz spats. Nonetheless, they have emerged triumphant, repeatedly crowned as one of rock's biggest saviours. How did they do it? Is it justified? Will they be able to maintain this lofty status? Read on ...

CHAPTER 1

Winners And Losers In Cool Britannia

"We were thinking about this yesterday – we were just sitting in a little room [at college], just writing songs all the time. And then three years later we can play them all over the world."

Chris Martin

It's the autumn of 1996, and music of wildly contrasting integrity clutters up the British charts. For those with discerning ears, there was the chart-topping 'Setting Sun' by The Chemical Brothers featuring Noel Gallagher, followed a few weeks later by 'Breathe', a hard dance masterpiece by the world-conquering Prodigy. Yet over in the album charts, the run-in to Christmas saw a terrifying sequence at the top, starting with Peter Andre, followed by Simply Red, Beautiful South, Boyzone, The Spice Girls and, more disturbing still, Robson & Jerome, chart-topping at Christmas for the second year in succession.

The year had started off well with Oasis' *(What's The Story) Morning Glory?*, a multi-platinum album and the logical commercial peak of the self-styled Britpop movement. Genealogically traceable through Suede's London-centric first album and still further back through the so-called

New Wave of New Wave bands, Britpop was a welcome respite from the slacker culture and US-dominated grunge years at the start of the decade. At its height, Britpop saw an 18-month heyday when Blur and Oasis were household names; Pulp finally broke their 14-year duck with the sexually subversive, comically seedy triumph *His 'n' Hers*; and Elastica, The Auteurs and the soon-to-be-global Radiohead were all making impacts. Supergrass' début album, *I Should Coco*, hit number one and a litany of other bands enjoyed purple patches as well, including Shed Seven, Portishead, The Bluetones, Marion, Dodgy and even a revived Modfather, Paul Weller, smiling benignly down on these young disciples who'd obviously listened hard to The Jam's back catalogue. It was good for business too, with live music experiencing a resurgence, band merchandise selling out and festivals enjoying renewed popularity.

By 1996, however, Britpop's foundations were crumbling. All was not well in the camp. The 'chart battle' between Oasis and the triumphant Blur the previous August had seen Britpop's commercial zenith but, paradoxically, its creative nadir. Despite their fleeting chart success, Blur soon took second place to Oasis' coming behemoth album, leaving Damon Albarn to shrink into a corner, reviled for the cartoon excesses of his band and distrusted for being Britpop's pretty boy. Within five years, the man who frolicked with Page Three stunners in the video for 'Country House' was recording world music with African instrumentalists. He would go on to experiment deeply both within Blur and, of course, with the critically revered and seminal multi-media band Gorillaz. His role in Britpop was over.

For the Gallaghers, 'Roll With It' was arguably their worst single ever, which Noel pretty much admitted in later interviews. Seeing both bands on *The Six O'Clock News* seemed a portent of halcyon days gone by. Britpop had been picked up by the media as a perfect counterpoint to the tiresome machismo – and corporate mutation – of grunge. Now, within two years of Kurt Cobain's suicide, Britpop had turned into the monster it had once despised. By mid-1996, with most of the big Britpop players recording new material or on sabbaticals, the movement was effectively dead.

A few survivors floated to the surface in the post-Britpop vacuum. Suede negotiated the loss of their guitarist and returned with *Coming*

Up, an album that may not have enjoyed the critical and commercial acclaim of previous records but was clearly their best effort to date. Manic Street Preachers were already well on the way to prolonged stadium status, though many felt this was achieved on the back of increasingly conservative output. Blur's forthcoming hardcore-inspired eponymous album was a dramatic shift in direction that firmly refuted their Britpop tag.

Britpop was never a transatlantic phenomenon. Ironic, quirky vignettes by bands like Blur, Suede, Bluetones, Supergrass, Pulp and a host of others meant nothing in America. Oasis enjoyed some *Billboard* success but this was diminished by unseemly tiffs between the brothers Gallagher and disrupted tours that prevented any real momentum being generated. Radiohead, almost throttled by the unexpected success of the anthem 'Creep', had pulled back from the brink with the delicious subtleties of *The Bends* but would not enjoy global popularity until the seismic impact of their pivotal *OK Computer*. Only The Prodigy, who entered the *Billboard* chart at number one with *The Fat Of The Land* (as they did in 23 other countries compared to *Morning Glory*'s 14) could boast truly international success but the Essex hard dance band fell way outside the shadow of Britpop.

What, pop-pickers wanted to know, would happen next?

★ ★ ★

"What was I like as a kid? The same as I am now, just smaller with a higher voice."

Chris Martin

It was against this backdrop, in the uneasy calm of the post-Britpop vacuum, that the four future members of Coldplay began to assemble. The notorious and seductive traction beam called London duly sucked these aspiring rock stars in, heady with dreams of stardom and musical acclaim.

Chris Martin was the eldest son of a chartered accountant father and a mother who taught biology. Born on March 3, 1977, he shares his birthday with Alexander Graham Bell, the inventor of the telephone.

That same month, A&M was reneging on the record deal it had famously signed with The Sex Pistols outside Buckingham Palace, a contract that so shocked Rick Wakeman that the caped Yes-man threatened to withdraw his labour. Punk captured the headlines while disco dominated the dance floor; artists like Donna Summer, Showaddywaddy, Hot Chocolate and The Muppets enjoyed far more commercial success than punk's angry firebrands.

The anti-establishment rants of London's punk inner circle were far removed from the sleepy Devonshire village of Whitestone, a few miles east of Exeter, where Chris was born. He was raised with his four siblings: two sisters and two brothers. In light of Chris's latter-day reputation as an almost puritanical abstainer, one of his brothers growing up to be a drum-and-bass DJ was comically contradictory: "(He is) the anti-Chris, the cool one (who has) experienced all these things for me." Prior to Chris, the nearest the Martin family had come to fame was his great-great-grandfather, William Willet, who invented British summertime. While riding his horse early each morning, Willet rued the fact that no one else was enjoying the sunshine and came up with the simple brainwave to move the clocks forward one hour.

The family home was large and set in luxurious grounds. Chris spent much of his childhood gazing out of sash windows across manicured lawns, and he makes no secret of the fact that he benefited from a first-class education. His secondary studies sent him to Sherborne boarding school in Yeovil, one of the country's finest public schools. A battered comprehensive this may not have been, but there was certainly no shortage of opportunities for creativity. Chris was a keen artist, but his primary love was always music. He had mixed tastes at this stage – the first single he bought was Blur's 'There's No Other Way' and the first album was Michael Jackson's 40-million seller, *Thriller*. He also had a penchant for The Pet Shop Boys and a smattering of soul classics.

Inevitably, his passion for listening to records evolved into a need to play music himself. In very early bands he played keyboards only alongside various school friends, bands subsequently identified as The Rockin' Honkies and The Red Rooster Boogie Band, who counted standards such as 'Mustang Sally' and 'Sitting On The Dock Of The Bay' as key tracks in their set.

Another early band was The Pet Shop Boys-influenced Identity Crisis. Although short-lived, this electro-pop outfit did provide one essential experience that Chris Martin would carry into his adulthood and career with Coldplay: being booed offstage. Chris had taken to the stage in a less-than-flattering leather waistcoat, video footage of which is said to be locked deep in some ex-pupil's wardrobe. However, his sartorial *faux pas* worsened with time. At one particular gig, Chris borrowed a long raincoat from a friend and enthusiastically aped the rock star antics of U2's frontman Bono. It went down like the proverbial lead balloon. Distraught, Chris vowed to only ever "be completely normal" from then on. Fortunately, all was not lost. Through a shared love of U2's *Zooropa*, Chris met Phil Harvey, Coldplay's future manager and 'fifth member' of the band. They quickly became close friends, and Chris even dated Phil's younger sister for a while.

Back at home, Chris's musical bent was readily encouraged by his father, although his dad later admitted that he was just humouring him in the hope that the phase would pass. Inadvertently of course, this just fuelled Chris's enthusiasm. In later years, Chris's father proved to be one of the band's biggest fans and his son's most sage advisor.

His father's encouragement was mirrored by an open-minded music teacher at Chris's school, Mr Tanner. "He dismissed the idea that you had to be some kind of miniature Mozart to enjoy music," Chris told Everette True. "He bought these Yamaha keyboards for the school, those PSS140s, about £100. They were very easy to work with, everyone could have a go. You could play with one finger and have a tune, so we did. That led to the first band I was in."

Outside of music, Chris's time at Sherbourne was largely unremarkable. The most troublesome period in his eyes was when, for a couple of years, he worried he was gay and fretted about the barracking and prejudice he might suffer: "I was 16 when I finally felt confident I wasn't [gay]. But the homophobia [at public school] can be pretty intense." There was even one time when he spotted a girl who he thought looked nice, but when she turned around it was a boy. "So I put on a deep voice and walked away!"

Probably the most controversial episode in Chris's otherwise sedate teenage years was when he and a friend stole a Mars Bar from Superdrug and got caught – he never did it again, so he was hardly a juvenile repeat offender. He was much happier reading Sherlock Holmes stories, surfing and listening to obscure classical piano music.

With the security of Coldplay's near-universal critical acclaim to ease his inner doubts, Chris can now be more forthright about his childhood years: "I hate apologising because as far as I'm concerned it was a privilege to have an amazing education. I had some incredible teachers, great facilities. What a privilege! But so what? Does anyone give a shit?"

Fife, Scotland-born Guy Berryman was the son of an engineer and, like Chris, also came from a stable household of means. The first dozen years of his childhood were spent in Kirkaldy, before a family relocation to Canterbury in Kent when he was 13. Like most primary school children, Guy started learning the recorder aged only eight, then progressed on to trumpet and finally, the year he moved to Kent, the bass. He began dabbling in numerous school bands, most notably the hideously named Time Out, an outfit that specialised in Genesis covers. "It was a guitar and keyboards band," he recalled. "We played terrible, terrible stuff. The best musician in the group was really into Genesis. We would agonise for hours trying to work out horrible prog rock stuff with ridiculous solos. We never got anywhere near it – we'd muck about and make a noise."

Time Out's questionable set list was in marked contrast to Guy's own musical preferences, which were decidedly funk and R&B-flavoured. He admits to having paid £100 for a rare vinyl copy of James Brown's *Hell* album only to see it re-issued on CD for £12 a few weeks later. "A bit annoying, but I did get an old Kool & The Gang compilation at a car-boot sale for 50p, which is worth £60. I just love that stuff, the rawness and the energy." He says his funk and soul collection was selected by follicle grandeur rather than musical preferences, with the young bassist primarily selecting most of his purchases by the size of Afro haircuts on the record sleeve.

Southampton-born Will Champion was the son of archaeology and music teacher parents and therefore a more adept musician than his future band cohorts, even at an early age. By his own admission, he was a far from ideal primary school pupil and ended up at a rough comprehensive for his secondary years. According to Will, fellow schoolmates 'graduated' to numerous prison sentences for, among other things, kicking somebody to death, GBH, arson and rape. So much for a privileged education. However, he believes he would have hated public school and feels the more abrasive environment at his school at least made him more street-wise.

The only known band from Will's childhood was called Fat Hamster. Will and two school friends called Iain and David formed this fleeting three-piece, but in their own words they were "absolute rubbish". They'd met at the Highfield Church activity group and were all local lads, so the idea of a band seemed perfectly natural. However, while Will eventually went off to join Coldplay, David grew up to be a successful drum-and-bass DJ while Iain played as wicket-keeper for Hampshire and then became goalkeeper at Totton FC.

Back then, the teenage Will was proficient on many different instruments, including the ever-useful tin whistle, so his latter-day decision to switch from guitar to drums was not as great a leap of faith as it might appear. "Will is like a human jukebox," explained Chris. "He knows more songs than anyone. You name it, he'll play it."

Jon Buckland came from Mold, a working-class area of Clywd in north Wales, whose chief rock 'n' roll claims to fame were former residents The Alarm, Karl Wallinger of World Party and Hollywood Brit-actor Rhys Ifans. Jon was born to a music-teacher mother and a biology/chemistry teacher father. Jon's father adored Eric Clapton and Jimi Hendrix so his son's future role in Coldplay is not surprising.

Jon can play the piano and harmonica (like Chris) and started learning guitar two years earlier than Guy, aged only 11. Jon's first guitar was a simple, budget, Japanese six-string. He tried to form bands pretty soon after he had mastered the rudiments of the instrument. One year prior to that, he'd formed an *ad hoc* rap band, but this outfit quickly mutated into a pop act, which was how he came to be interested in guitar. Aged 13 he also began guitar lessons with a local expert called Jan Beck. Jonny could lay claim to perhaps the most critically acceptable of childhood influences, preferring guitar bands such as The Stone Roses and Ride.

Add to the mix a splice of his older brother's My Bloody Valentine and Sonic Youth records and the young guitarist already had an intriguing blend of influences. The first two records he recalls buying were rather less impressive: a Beautiful South single and the mega-mix musical horror that was the chart-topping Jive Bunny & The Master Mixers. His early teenage years were mostly a mass of badly drawn album covers for nonexistent bands with increasingly corny names. One heavy metal band that did make it to actual rehearsals played a bizarre cover of Madness' classic 'Night Boat To Cairo'.

The hub of Coldplay's genesis was University College, London. The product of four decidedly (and unashamedly) unbroken homes, the future members of Coldplay all headed for the central London school with fiery aspirations for a bright future: "[We all had] real Dick Whittington-type ambitions," admitted Chris in *NME*. "Go to London, make your fortune. Well, sort of. And when you go to college you've got a clean slate, no-one knows who you are and you've kind of decided pretty much who you want to be."

Will enrolled for an anthropology course (his archaeologist father was once described by Chris as "the Michael Jackson of archaeology"); Jon opted for maths and astronomy; Guy followed in his father's science footsteps by studying engineering, although he later switched to architecture; for Chris, the process was a little more protracted. At first he applied to another college to study English but was politely informed that his stated wish, as submitted on his application form, that he wanted to improve his written language "to help with my lyrics" was not what they were looking for. Eventually, Chris ended up at UCL studying ancient history.

The first freshers' week saw Chris and Jon become acquainted around the Students' Union pool table. They quickly became friends and shared a common interest in music, albeit Sting and a then-disco obsessed and critically chided U2. The other music Chris began to hear at UCL was a revelation, however, and before long he was tumbling into the expressive vocals and staggering range of the late Jeff Buckley. In turn, Buckley's renowned diversity in his selection of covers led Chris into buying albums by artists as varied as Leonard Cohen and Elkie Brooks. Closer to home, the increasingly perplexing yet utterly compelling genius of Radiohead was also a regular on the stereo during Chris and Jon's late night halls of residence hang-outs, as were epic throwbacks from the likes of Echo & The Bunnymen.

Undeterred by the lack of a full band or any live experience together, the duo immediately started writing original material. "Meeting Jonny was like falling in love. He could make all the ideas work and we were writing two songs a night sometimes." Jon was reciprocally impressed: "From the moment I met Chris, I really did think that we could go all the way."

For the next nine months, Chris and Jon toyed with formally starting a band, cobbling together snippets of songs and ideas for music while all the time continuing their studies. Rumour has it that Chris was even formulating a boy band as his route to musical glory, an outfit whose name – Pectoralz – promised little in the way of Grammy-winning creative genius (fortunately, this 'concept' pop band never actually performed or rehearsed). Events soon took a turn that would ensure Pectoralz remained just a bad pipe dream: legend has it that fellow UCL student and funk-obsessed bassist Guy Berryman heard of Chris and Jon's embryonic compositions and confronted them in the student bar, inebriatedly demanding to be allowed to join their 'band'. "We couldn't really say no," recalls Jon. Chris thought that Guy was a little scary when they first met but now says he is much nicer than he appears, being softly spoken rather than moody, albeit still the "quiet" member of Coldplay.

Shortly after, Guy dropped out of his engineering course, opting instead for a degree in architecture that was supposed to span a full seven years. He eventually pulled out of that too but chose to stay in London to see how this new band with Chris and Jon worked out (leaving Guy as the only non-graduate in the band). Just as well, because by the time he would have finished the seven-year course and begun the lucrative work of being a qualified architect, he was already part of one of the biggest bands on the planet with a clutch of Brits, two Grammys and millions of records sold.

All three bandmates lived in UCL's Ramsey Hall, their close proximity to each other making it easy to strum guitars and write songs whenever it took their fancy. With a student aplomb that would appall their later critics, the trio would often find themselves playing Simon & Garfunkel songs in the stairwells of the halls of residence.

The final piece of the Coldplay jigsaw was the arrival of Will Champion. The nature of his recruitment as permanent drummer was quite the opposite to that of the overtly enthusiastic bassist Guy. The trio of Chris, Jon and Guy knew of a reputable drummer at UCL and approached him with a crude demo of some nascent songs of theirs, which included a very early version of Coldplay's eventual début album opener, 'Don't Panic'. "We played him 'Panic' and he said, 'No'. We just couldn't believe it. Even then there was a feeling of, 'But what we're doing is great. Why wouldn't you want to be part of it?'"

One day, Chris was recounting this rejection to his hockey team-mate and casual acquaintance, Will Champion. Will informed Chris that his room-mate was also a drummer and offered to set up a rehearsal. The problem was, when the three arrived at Will's digs, the drummer was nowhere to be seen. Anxious not to have wasted their time, Will suggested that, although he was actually an aspiring guitarist, maybe he could keep basic time behind the kit and they could rehearse anyway. With the absent drummer down the local pub, Will thus found himself enrolled as Coldplay's sticksman. The date was January 6, 1998. Initially, Will actually played guitar in the line-up but gradually his equal prowess behind the drums saw him take up that role more permanently. "He was a better drummer than me," Jonny later told *The Times-Picayune*. "He probably is a better guitarist – he's a very good guitarist. He's pretty much good at everything he does. He can even play the tin whistle. He's sort of a multi-talented, Swiss Army drummer."

Chris and Will would often jam on guitar together. One day, the two friends had been playing and decided that, since they were broke, they would travel into central London and busk for money. At the time they had grand visions of playing to increasingly large crowds as the money piled up in ever-more bulging hats at their feet. As it turned out, they played a Beatles track and 'Mrs Robinson', followed by a song from *The Jungle Book*, to about six people, earning only 20 pence before being moved on by the police.

★

Coldplay "borrowed" their name from a fellow student who no longer wanted to use the moniker because he felt it was "too depressing". Just as well, as alternative names that had been mooted were Stepney Green or Starfish – there are unsubstantiated rumours of the foursome playing a gig in Camden using the latter name, but they would later confirm that although actual gigs *were* booked and rehearsals completed, no shows were ever played under this moniker.

The first ever 'official' Coldplay song was a novelty number called 'Ode To Deodorant', compiled in Jon's bedroom. At this stage, it wasn't just their songs that were far from rock star material: Chris was shy, lanky and wore a tooth brace, hardly a 19-year-old potential Kurt Cobain.

Will proved more than just a useful stand-in drummer. He handed over his blue Telecaster to Jon, and the same guitar went on to provide the backbone to many Coldplay songs. Then, within a few days of stumbling into the band, he arranged a gig at the now-defunct Laurel Tree in Camden, north London. Among the six-song set, nervously aired to a modest crowd made up almost entirely of college mates, were two songs, 'Don't Panic' and 'High Speed', which – suitably honed – would make it on to their eventual début album. Quite how these ethereal ballads, in particular the softly spoken chimes of the latter, came across over the house PA of a small pub is lost in the mists of time. Yet even in Coldplay's infancy, Chris recalls that the band had grand designs that made no countenance for failure: "There was no Plan B."

CHAPTER 2

Safety In Numbers

With the world's attention drawn to the football World Cup in France, Coldplay began to develop their masterplan. First priority was songwriting, closely followed by almost daily rehearsals in bathrooms, cellars, bedrooms, and even one wind-swept session in a local park. The band's manager arrived courtesy of a mix-up over a gig. They had arranged to play at Dingwalls in Camden, persuading the venue to put two friends' bands on the bill as well. Coachloads of mates were chaperoned to come to the show and Coldplay spent weeks avidly rehearsing.

Then two weeks before the actual gig, it became clear there had been a big mix-up. There were actually going to be eight bands on the bill, Coldplay were on fifth and would play for only 15 minutes. They would get no door money and just 10p for each flyer handed in with their name on it.

Chris had kept in touch with his friend Phil Harvey, a fellow pupil at Sherbourne, and so in the midst of this impending disaster, the singer asked him outright to be their manager. Phil agreed and immediately phoned up Dingwalls to cancel the gig. He then cleverly hired out the same venue – with his own money – the night after Coldplay had originally been booked. Not only that, he offered to pay for the band to go into a tiny studio called Sync City, in Tottenham, to record their first demo.

The princely sum of £1,500 was needed for this first recording. It was spring 1998 and the singles charts were peppered with the likes of Aqua, Boyzone, B★Witched and All Saints. Massive Attack had just enjoyed a number one with their 'comeback' album, *Mezzanine*, but otherwise the British music scene was largely unrewarding.

The product of this début studio session was *The Safety EP*. It contained three tracks, the subtle swagger of 'Bigger Stronger', 'No More Keeping My Feet On The Ground' and 'Such A Rush'. All three songs had Jon's trademark ringing guitars and Chris's gentle voice, but this was very much a less refined version of Coldplay than would be found on later records. Still, it was a strong opening salvo intended merely as a sampler for record companies and music industry only. Interestingly, the name of the EP actually comes from the sleeve itself – the cover photograph was a long exposure shot of Chris standing under a doorway 'safety' sign.

By now, Phil Harvey had taken to the role of band manager with a passion and worked relentlessly to spread the gospel with this début release. Without an orthodox record deal or even a self-distribution deal, the limited edition of only 500 copies of *The Safety EP* was destined for the record collections of friends and a few select members of the media and record business. It is now one of the most sought-after releases for any Coldplay record collector, with scarce copies occasionally appearing on internet auction sites for in excess of £150. Jonny took versions of the EP tracks to Jan Beck, his former guitar teacher, who was very open in the press with his opinion: "He brought the band's first EP to me and I said you won't get very far with this – technically it wasn't very well recorded."

At this point, gigs were scarce, especially throughout the football-obsessed summer months of 1998. What gigs they did secure invariably ended up in chaos. Coldplay performed at Wye Farming College's end of term ball, billed as support to then-chart regulars Space. Countless technical problems meant Space eventually played *first* at 11pm, followed by two other bands before Coldplay finally took to the stage at 3am. By this time, most people were either blind drunk or dog-tired. One member of the audience kept getting up on stage and dancing alongside the band, before returning to his corner of the room for another swig of watery student beer.

Coldplay's next live disaster was at Manchester's unsigned band festival, 'In The City'. This September gig at the Cuban Café got off to a bad start when Chris left his guitar pedals in Devon. Phil did a spot of quick thinking and arranged for a long-distance lorry driver he knew to take the pedals up to Manchester as part of his route. Coldplay were the first band on at the minuscule venue, circumstances made worse by a dreadful sound system. Chris forgot the words to the first song and matters went downhill from there on.

All of these early live experiences were solicited by *The Safety EP*. Although they were far from enjoyable, they were an essential part of the band's apprenticeship. On December 7, 1998, however, the EP secured them a gig that would prove to be pivotal. The show was at the Camden Falcon pub, a small but legendary venue that had seen famously crammed gigs by the likes of Suede, Blur, PJ Harvey and many others 'before they were famous'. The pub was a regular haunt for record company A&R men.

However, almost a lone industry figure at the Falcon that night was Simon Williams, sometime music journalist and now founder of the independent record label, Fierce Panda. He told the author about how he came to sign Coldplay for a single deal after having seen this show: "I got *The Safety EP* after I'd seen them play live at that Falcon show. I'd love to give it some sexy A&R spin and say there was something in the wind that said I must go to this gig and see this band, but we had the same lawyer! He had been working with them for a few months and he knew they were sitting on something really special, and BMG publishing were all over it as well, but they couldn't convince any record companies of the band's merit. It was kind of like the last throw of the dice really, and it was only really an aside about the future of Fierce Panda that he mentioned the fact they were playing. I almost went along as a favour. I thought they were brilliant and the turnout was impressive too; so was the vibe and the songs."

Williams refutes the linear notion that Coldplay simply formed, became the subject of a bidding frenzy and were then quickly signed. "This is how it all gets rewritten with these bands. I can't even say that the majors had really passed on them, because they didn't even have a big In The City showcase [that year]; apparently there were only about four labels there who saw them that year in Manchester. Coldplay didn't fit in with anything. At the time they probably had a lot more negative responses than positive ones; if you did ask anyone's opinion of Coldplay, they'd say they were ripping off Radiohead and they were ripping off Jeff Buckley. At that point those were two of the most sacred talents in the music industry. Some people found it a little bit insulting; it was a fairly intense experience to see Buckley or Radiohead live and it wasn't intense going to see Coldplay, because Chris was a bit knockabout, a bit jokey and a bit flirty, so I think a good few people did find that insulting. There was still a little bit of a mixed opinion." Nonetheless Williams had named the band as one of his tips for success in the New Year's edition of *NME*, despite still being unsigned. Anyone intrigued by his festive tip-off was able to see them play live during a New Year smattering of small pub circuit shows in January, including two dates at the Bull & Gate in Kentish Town. It was an exciting time to be going to gigs in London – other 'unknown' bands causing a stir at this time were Muse and Elbow.

And much like the fabled Sex Pistols show in 1976 at Manchester Free Trade Hall (when about 5,000 people claim to have seen the nascent punks' show, when in fact research proves there were less than 30 people in the audience), the Coldplay gig at the Falcon was similarly different from how history now depicts it. The show was busy, but not with salivating record labels: "There was no industry there at all," recalls Williams. "I had a good old look around, that's what you do, because most of the time [when a band's coming up] there's 10 real people in the crowd and the rest is music industry. Coldplay was the exact opposite. I personally can't remember a single A&R person who was there. I remarked on that to the band and told them they had an amazing fan base there, but they said they weren't fans, 'they are just our mates'. I said as far as I was concerned if they were applauding and cheering that's beyond being a mate – it's one thing to turn up and give you a bit of support, but another to actively enjoy and sing along to the entire bloody set! They had the mighty power of the students too, the ULU thing. The Falcon was probably a 176-person sell-out. Really impressive on every possible level."

Excited by the performance, Williams decided to approach the band there and then. "It was a dream really, something that try as you might to replicate nowadays, you just couldn't do it. Of course, you can always walk up to an unknown band playing to about 20 people, but nine times out of 10 they are absolutely appalling! That night I just thought, 'Strike while the iron's hot' – this was before email, so the way of communicating was *mano a mano* backstage right after the gig. Or in the case of the Falcon, down the corridor. So I got straight in there and said, 'Would you like to do a single?' Most of the time these people are so shocked by the approach that they say 'yes'! And that's exactly what Coldplay did."

Williams' memory of the four unknown musicians remains very positive: "Really affable, just fun, they knew they had played a great gig, they knew they were a great band, and they were popular individuals regardless of the music they were playing. They were confident young bucks. Financially I presume they weren't having a terribly hard time because they came from fairly decent families, and it was kind of a blast. This was even though they hadn't been getting much love from major labels, and they certainly weren't getting much love from other indie labels. How many indie labels would have signed something like that? McGee for Creation? Rough Trade? Not gonna work. Beggars? Maybe... don't really know. We were the only indie that was capable of doing 'uncool' bands like Coldplay primarily because we have never pretended to be cool."

Having a single out on such a revered label was a massive leap forward for Coldplay. "We had the normal thing of Christmas killing everything for a short while, so we took it easy. The great thing was that Coldplay didn't rush anything. We put them into Station Studios in Southgate right by the tube with a man called Mike Beever. A great producer – coincidentally we liked the idea of having a man with an animal name working with us at Fierce Panda (and not for any rude reason!). In they went with Mike. Jolly good fun, 400 quid on three songs. Coupla days all in for the whole kaboodle. A bargain then and a bargain today!" 'Brothers & Sisters', backed with 'Easy To Please' and 'Only Superstition', was released in April, 1999. Only 2,500 copies were pressed.

"Next up was plotting," explains Simon Williams, "bringing them under the gigging umbrella for us, putting the team together and generally going to the pub with them. They lived in a student gaff near where I lived, so we'd go to Camden and drink and talk about life."

It wasn't just the modest funds for recording that Fierce Panda provided. Simon Williams is widely revered as a taste-maker supreme and therefore if he has championed a band – almost regardless of their sound and background – industry ears will be pricked. In his time, he has released very early (and often first) records by the likes of Keane, Ash, Supergrass and Death Cab For Cutie. In other words, this is a man whose opinion you listen to.

"The key factor apart from [the release]," continues Williams, "was being the first cog in the machine. We happened to be the first people to put the record out and give it some kind of authority. Then that went to *NME* and then Radio 1 and then Steve Lamacq got hold of it really quickly and it sounded great on the radio. There you are: the single's coming out in three months' time, you are on Radio 1, you are all over *NME*, bish bosh! It transformed everything in three months. At that first Bull & Gate gig, they'd played to about 70 people; by March it was absolutely rammed and sold out, people were crying because they couldn't get in, major label A&R people were crying. They weren't actual tears, mind…

"The single gave a pretty good indication of where they were headed," opines Williams. "They were never fans of the recording though. They were always very much a major label band. They are just moderately embarrassed [looking back on the EP] I think." Nonetheless, at the time the record's more accomplished sound soon began to make ripples in the music business. For a start, the band enjoyed their first music press reviews, most notably perhaps in *NME*, who said the song "has a clear eye and an honest face. The youth-group outreach projects await." At this point, Steve Lamacq's sadly missed BBC Radio 1 *Evening Session* was at its prime and as Williams pointed out he played the lead track heavily. The single even pierced the official charts, albeit at a lowly number 92, but this was a very good progression for only Coldplay's second ever studio session. Simon Williams remembers that, "When it charted, the band were absolutely overjoyed!" ('Brothers & Sisters' later appeared on the so-called *The Dead Cheap Fierce Panda* sampler and also as the B-side for later single 'Trouble'.)

Unbeknown to Coldplay at this time, one big-hitting A&R man was closely on their trail, a copy of *The Safety EP* having landed on his desk a few weeks after its initial release. Dan Keeling was a recently appointed talent scout for Parlophone, part of the EMI group that at the time also released Radiohead, Blur, The Beatles, Kylie and Geri Halliwell. Suitably curious, Keeling had gone to see the band play a pre-Christmas 1998 gig at Cairo Jack's, an Egyptian-themed pub just off Regents Street in the West End of London. The venue was small, the crowd even smaller. "I wasn't really that enamoured," Keeling later told *Q* magazine. "I thought Chris had something. He was quite charismatic. But the sound wasn't there."

Undeterred, by the time Keeling heard the 'Brothers & Sisters' single, he was already considering making an offer to the band. His interest was shared by that of Caroline Elleray at BMG Music Publishing who was also alerted to the band by the début EP and who later signed them to a publishing contract (Caroline is widely acknowledged as a major player in the band's success).

With three members of Coldplay still at college, many in the record business viewed *The Safety EP* and the 'Brothers & Sisters' single as a temporary hobby by students on the verge of 'proper' careers. In a climate when record deals were becoming increasingly scarce, with the already exorbitant cost of launching a new band on the rise, any group who might not be unconditionally committed seemed a risk not worth taking. Fierce Panda's Simon Williams was unfettered by this concern and was busy trying to formulate a plan that meant he could sign the band to his indie label: "We tried to sign them to [partner label] Mushroom because we had a deal there at the time. Coldplay would have been our first big hit band."

Eventually, in the late spring of 1999, an enthusiastic Dan Keeling made his move and contacted the band. He was particularly impressed with 'No More Keeping My Feet On The Ground', as he told *Q*: "It just overwhelmed me. I wanted to stay cool but I could only hold off calling [them] until Saturday morning. I met Phil, but Chris couldn't come because he was doing his exams." Once other labels had registered Parlophone's interest, something of a cheque book scrum ensued but Keeling triumphed and eventually signed the band for an eight-album deal. Simon Williams had no hard feelings when he heard the news:

"They chose Parlophone. Every other major label under the sun had suddenly woken up and realised what they were missing out on. I know that Parlophone was enticing – from the band's perspective they adored [Parlophone band] Radiohead and that label was incredibly strong at the time. Back then they were joining a brilliant stable: Supergrass, Mansun, Radiohead were all enormous, it seemed like the perfect place for them and if I had been Coldplay I'd have probably signed to Parlophone too. And let's face it, we can't really say [that label] didn't do a good job! No hard feelings though, we gave it our best shot."

Fortunately, the three members of Coldplay who were still studying came up trumps in their June 1999 final exams. Despite all the exciting musical distractions, Chris earned a first-class degree, while both Jon and Will scored 2:1s. The actual signing of the record contract took place in the centre of London's Trafalgar Square, only a mile away from where The Sex Pistols posed with their A&M contract outside Buckingham Palace in 1977. The fun continued when they signed their publishing deal on a rowing boat in the middle of the Serpentine in Hyde Park. "We only had enough money for 15 minutes (on the boat) so we had to do it sharpish!" said Chris.

The euphoric mood quickly faded. With a début Parlophone release scheduled for early winter of 1999, Coldplay's own obligations and the expectations of the record company hit the band like a truck. They were sent to record an EP with Beta Band producer Chris Allison, to be called *The Blue Room EP*, but found the reality of the experience very different from the glamorous ideal most aspiring bands imagine. They were rising early to get to the studio, taking the crowded London Underground in 90-degree heat to the studio based in the grimy, crime-ridden Elephant and Castle area of south London. The discomfort of their commute alongside millions of other nine-to-fivers was exacerbated by a summer of train delays and industrial disputes.

On top of it all, when they got to the studio, progress wasn't always swift. Chris Allison had indeed made a celebrated name for himself working with the likes of The Wedding Present and The Beta Band. Chris spoke to the author for this book and explained why these first major label sessions were not always straightforward. "The guys had just finished college at UCL and they were suddenly flung into a major recording contract where a number of labels had been pitching for them, the expectations were high, so they probably felt a lot of pressure. They were fairly green when it came to being in the studio and one of the main tasks I had been hired for was to get more of a unique 'sound' out of the band. When a gigging band comes to a producer there's usually some sort of identifiable sound to capture that has been honed down through gigging and/or rehearsals. With Coldplay there was something of a sound, but not something that was perfected in any particular way or that the band or label were necessarily happy with.

"Artists such as the Wedding Present or The Beta Band have their own defining sound and as a producer you are really refining it and making a good recording of it, making the odd suggestion here and there for arrangement or instrument ideas. It's more like icing on the cake. With Coldplay they just needed something that was going to work and be unique to them. However, in hindsight I think maybe the direction that I was going didn't gel as well as they would have liked. I think we did seven tracks together (of which some were unreleased)."

Chris had previously seen Coldplay live and therefore knew that their frontman had a presence, but in his opinion matters in the studio were less clear: "I thought that they were talented at songwriting and Chris had a great voice and presence, but I didn't necessarily feel that there was a honed down and unique band sound."

The expectations of their freshly signed record deal and the fact that after all the dreaming they were now in a professional studio, funded by a major label who expected results, rapidly took its toll, and on Chris Martin in particular. He openly admits that the ticking of the corporate clock ground him down very quickly and he lashed out at the band – and Will – in particular. As he recounted in Q magazine, "Things were going wrong in the studio and I told Will it was his fault. He'd be out of time once and I'd be telling him he was shit."

Not surprisingly, Will wouldn't stand for this and walked out. It would be a full, anxious week before the situation was remedied and Coldplay were back in business: "And it was all my fault," admitted Chris. "I thought to myself, 'You fucking twat'. I was so nervous of us fucking up our chance I'd become obsessed with whether we were a technically good band or not. I apologised, but I felt I had to pay, so I got drunk." Chris remains a non-smoker and very moderate drinker, so it was all the more peculiar that he decided to punish himself by getting blind drunk. Filling his previously alcohol-free body with lashings of beer, vodka and, oddly enough, Ribena, Chris's self-destruct ended in a paralytic and uncomfortable stupor. Guy was in his own flat when Chris began the bender and chose to go out with his girlfriend, returning to find Chris dribbling Ribena-laced vomit on the floor. "He's not been drunk since," says Guy. "Chris brings quite enough spice to our lives without alcohol being involved. When his energy is up he's brilliant. Creatively he's great. But when the energy is down, it makes things tough. That was a horrible time which I could never go through again."

"Unfortunately with a drummer," continues producer Chris Allison, "you are either in time or you are out of time with whatever feel you are going for. It is pretty important for a drummer to lock down the basis of the track, otherwise you are laying the rest of the instruments on shifting sand, as opposed to something that is coherent. I will just add that drum issues make a producer's life very difficult, because you really have to have the drums as solid as possible, otherwise things can go awfully wrong later on. The band probably didn't realise the extent to which they can go wrong, because they were inexperienced in the studio. So a lot of time was spent on the drums and we had to do a lot of dropping in and a lot of talking through, practicing and what not. That definitely put a strain on the sessions, which is a shame really, because they started off well." It only later transpired to the producer, however, that the band's drummer had very grave family worries: "I had no idea that Will's mother was very ill and I actually wish someone had told me, because he must have been under a lot of pressure. I put him under quite a lot of pressure as well, because it was taking so long to get good drum takes. I got on well with Chris, but things started to take their course and he probably got anxious that the session was running into difficulty, thinking about this big record deal, what's going to happen if they messed up? All these things were probably going through his mind and probably made him more stressed."

Coldplay only had those seven songs completed after several weeks of fractious recording sessions, most notably 'Don't Panic', 'See You Soon' and 'High Speed'. After a short break, producer Allison met up with them once more. "They wanted me to work on the album, firstly taking a break to write more material. When we reconvened a few months later at a rehearsal room to start the album proper, they weren't playing particularly well, they didn't seem to be getting on and they needed more time to pull it together. I just told them, for good or for bad, that I did not feel they were ready to go in and make the album yet, that they needed more rehearsal time. I guess I was cutting my own throat to a certain extent, but if I was going to do my job properly, I was going to have to be straight with them.

"The band were not particularly pleased, and I can understand that. They did go away and obviously they did spend the time getting it together. I don't know how long it was before they went back in the studio to make the album proper [with another producer], but by that time they'd come up with some new tracks, like 'Yellow'. Maybe I pushed them to make a better album, who knows, it's all history, they pulled themselves together and took the time to make a solid album ... it was extremely well received, so good on 'em!"

On reflection, Chris Martin's drunken interlude during these tempestuous début sessions was a defining watershed for the band. Suitably humbled, Chris vowed to tone down his rather puritanical control of Coldplay. It later came to light that 'band rules' included the protocol that anyone caught taking cocaine would face immediate dismissal.

More importantly perhaps, Chris declared that from that moment on, the band was a democratic group of four equal parts. Wisely, Chris decided that all future songwriting credits would be split four ways as would all income. This was in line with the policy favoured by other masters of longevity, including R.E.M. and U2. In R.E.M. Michael Stipe writes all the words, as does Bono in U2, yet both share all monies equally with the other three members. Industry insiders suggest this decision, which has surely been central to the founder members lasting over 20 years together, may have personally cost Bono in excess of £30 million. The question is, would they have even got past their first few albums had he – or in Coldplay's case, Chris – been earning far more than his colleagues? Rock 'n' roll is a volatile environment at the best of times, but when you add personal resentment over vastly differing incomes to the powder keg, the results are often terminal. In light of numerous famous and acrimonious legal battles (Spandau Ballet, Procul Harem *et al*) Chris said, "Do I really want to spend two weeks in court some way down the line arguing with my closest mates about who wrote what?"

CHAPTER 3

Harvest Festivals And The Feeding Of The 100,000

Coldplay gigged prolifically at this early stage of their career, with perhaps their most notable showing on the New Bands stage at the Glastonbury Festival in June of 1999. Organiser Michael Eavis once said of his legendary weekend event that, "I regarded the whole thing as a cross between a harvest festival and a pop festival." The festival in Worthy Farm, Pilton, Wiltshire had long since established itself as the greatest annual British outdoor music event of them all.

Although the early drug-addled, free-loving, hippified image of the oft-troubled festival was a million miles from Coldplay's own personal outlook, Glastonbury's origins were actually far more in keeping with their simple approach to rock 'n' roll. In the autumn of 1970, farmer Eavis booked the very first festival on his land near Glastonbury entirely on his own with no prior knowledge of the music business. The Kinks headlined and were paid £500. In modern times, the same headline slot would cost him £500,000. At that first Glastonbury festival, Eavis handed out free milk and provided a large ox roast (which was eaten by hungry Hells Angels). He still lost £1,500. Over the ensuing years, the festival became the granddaddy of the British weekender, equally well known for its muddy fields, frequently disgusting toilets and torrential rain as it is for top music. For aspiring and, indeed, high-profile bands, a slot at Glastonbury remains a huge coup.

Few students can boast playing at Glastonbury Festival just weeks after their final exams but that is exactly what happened to Coldplay. Their appearance on the New Band stage saw them deliver a polished, albeit slightly apprehensive performance. With the increasingly numerous record industry whispers about the band's potential, they attracted their fair share of journalists in the crowd on that day.

The performance brought one member of Coldplay full circle. In the early Nineties, Will had got a job working at the festival. That year, one of the main attractions was the Godfather of Soul, James Brown. Running around in the production area, word went round that Brown was proving a difficult star to accommodate. In the crackly ear-pieces of the production staff, an exasperated voice fizzled over the airwaves Brown's latest alleged requirements: "James Brown is refusing to go onstage until he has 25 Tommy Hilfiger rucksacks and a silk carpet to stand on." Laughing to himself, Will was not to know at that point that several years later, he would be on the New Band stage at the same festival. And when they played their 1999 show, Coldplay, in turn, were not to know that within two years they would be headlining.

The tricky sessions that Chris Allison had negotiated needed to be supplemented in order to flesh out the band's forthcoming *The Blue Room EP* on Parlophone, so both the previously recorded *Safety EP* tracks 'Bigger Stronger' and 'Such A Rush' were added to the track listing.

While recording the EP, Coldplay supported Welsh popsters Catatonia at The London Forum in Kentish Town. Lead singer Cerys Matthews was enjoying a spell as both a *bête noir* and home-grown darling of the music press, but her band were destined to spiral into an unseemly disintegration only a few months later. For now, this support slot was an excellent opportunity for Coldplay, their biggest indoor gig to date. At this stage, Chris was still a little star-struck by it all, telling *Guitarist* that: "I had to hold [Cery's] cigarette while she went to the loo!" The size of the venue and the scale of the production stuck in their minds: "That was incredible, it was huge," recalled Chris in *Select*. "It was one of our best gigs and we were amazed at the size of their rider. They had JD and tequila, it really gave us something to aspire to."

Simon Williams of Fierce Panda is keen to point out that despite latter-day critics often lampooning Coldplay as a 'soft' band, at this early stage of their career they did actually gig relentlessly. "That was their background, that's what they did. They never complained about any of the shows. They'd simply say, 'Of course we will play that gig, if you think it is a good idea, we'll do it'. No great strategy, just constant, constant gigging. I think that made them better human beings. It was real first-hand experience."

The Blue Room EP was a little grandiose perhaps, but nonetheless boded well for future records, suggesting a natural instinct for the epic. Both anthemic and folky, the five songs successfully mixed slithers of several styles. Most notable was the evolution of Chris's vocals, which were becoming stronger by the day. It was released in November 1999 in a run of 5,000 copies. The stakes were getting gradually higher.

This more high-profile release opened the band up to their first real taste of press criticism. A prophetic *NME* continued to champion them, saying the EP "hinted at the band's potential for stadium-destined greatness with a wholly civilised and occasionally dramatic take on the Radiohead/Jeff Buckley melancholic acoustic method of mass seduction." However, universal acclaim was by no means theirs, with many detractors chiding them for being overblown and, most commonly of all, miserabilists. This accusation was fiercely denied: "All our songs have very simple emotions," parried a defensive, albeit honest, Chris. "They're either very happy or very sad, but never miserable… Oh, all right, the last track, 'Such A Rush', is pretty damn depressing. But the rest aren't, I promise!"

Steve Lamacq's support at Radio 1 was substantial enough, but when Jo Whiley joined in the campaign, momentum really started to gather. Whiley had originally teamed up with Lamacq on the *Evening Session* but her 'promotion' to a daytime show meant her profile was far higher at that time. This nationwide daytime coverage for *The Blue Room EP* was complemented by heavy rotation on London's alternative radio station Xfm, which, although it couldn't boast the listenership of Radio 1, was seen as a credible source of new music nonetheless.

This rising profile coincided perfectly with the band's first nationwide tour, co-headlining with Icelandic band Bellatrix. This set of dates, their first trip out on the road for more than a couple of weeks, was boosted by a show at Liverpool's Royal Court, supporting critics' faves Gomez and the excellent Guided By Voices. At this stage, their motivation and aims were charmingly pure: "It's exciting," said Chris. "You put that bit extra into playing for a crowd who don't know you and your music. We always try and make an impression. We just want to get our music across."

Having spent December back at home, the band opened 2000 with a slot on the blitzkrieg '*NME* Premier Tour' alongside Campag Velocet, Shack and Les Rhythmes Digitales. Fortunately, Chris's pre-tour predictions that they would be playing to empty venues proved far from accurate. With the sponsorship of *NME*, the band was bound to enjoy great coverage. It was an important challenge for Coldplay, not least because this was the first time they had played a longer series of bigger venues and larger crowds.

Hard to imagine then, that at the start of the new millennium Coldplay were visibly "over the moon" to be playing Newcastle University; by the end of that same year, just under 12 months later, they would be the proud owners of a multi-million selling début album and a tour schedule that would in future only be able to be accommodated by the world's biggest arenas and stadiums.

CHAPTER 4

Turning Up The Heat

As yet, however, Coldplay had not even had a Top 40 hit. All that was about to change with their March, 2000, release of the single 'Shiver'.

Unfortunately, just as with *The Blue Room EP*, the sessions for this release were far from easy. Dan Keeling later admitted to being very disappointed by the first demos that were sent up to him in London from the band's base at the Rockfield studios in south Wales. He was so concerned that the sublime energy of their live show was nowhere to be seen, he got straight in his car and headed off down the M4 to confront the band. He met with a predictably cold response. It was then that he first fully realised the extent of the renowned close-knit clique that the four band members maintain to this day. "They don't like people sticking their noses in," he said.

The band recorded 'Shiver' using an analogue desk, rather than the feted and fashionable hi-tech digital desks so commonplace in the modern studio. Both vocals and guitars were redubbed on more than one occasion in the search for perfection. Smaller parts of the three-song release were also completed at Liverpool's Parr Street Studios. Notably, both for this song and 'For You', Chris's guitar was detuned to make some of the more complex chord sequences easier to achieve. One of the B-sides, 'For You', was recorded against the grain in just one night and under pressure for results. This duo of songs was complemented by an acoustic version of 'Careful Where You Stand'.

The lead song, 'Shiver', was actually written two years prior to its eventual release. In a rare explanation of a song, some reports suggested Chris wrote the track while thinking about Natalie Imbruglia, a statement that he later vehemently denied. Closer inspection suggests that the ex-*Neighbours* starlet may have not been the inspiration; instead the fuel for Chris's muse appears more likely to have been the fact that he enjoyed little success with girlfriends throughout his teens and early twenties.

Chris admitted that the single was effectively something of a stalking song and comparisons have been made to Otis Lee Crenshaw's classic country number, 'Women Call It Stalking (It's Just Selective Walking)'. He wrote the track during a glum period when he felt he might never find the right partner, something "most blokes do". He finally revealed the song was about a specific girl and that he believes that the woman in question knows it is about her.

He was painfully reluctant to reveal too much however. When promoting this single, he complained that he found it difficult, even pointless, to pontificate about the meaning of his songs: "I just find all this really funny. It's just a song. I've got nothing to say about these songs."

Inevitably, given the nature of the transcendent vocals and dark undercurrent to 'Shiver', comparisons to Jeff Buckley abounded. With refreshing honesty, Chris had no problem discussing this theory with A Beautiful World's reporter: "That song *is* a direct nod to Jeff Buckley. I certainly was listening to nothing but Jeff Buckley when we wrote that song... so, yeah, it's the most blatant rip-off song, but it's still a good song, and that's why we kept it. [But] he would have done it better!"

Buckley was not the only artist to whom Coldplay were repeatedly being compared. Already whispers of 'this year's Travis' were circulating and, perhaps more accurately, the band was coming under increasing attack for being apparent Radiohead imitators. Although rather uncharitable (and largely inaccurate), it is easy to see why some might suggest this. The stinging guitar of a Coldplay chorus often contrasted sharply with the much softer moods of the verse, while controlled falsetto was complemented by full-tilt vocals, a Chris Martin vocal trait used right from the very beginnings of his interest in music. 'Shiver' was definitely a Coldplay song, not a Radiohead tribute, but this was a comparison that would simply not go away (more of which later).

Whatever the inspiration behind the single, it was probably the first real sign that Coldplay had it in them to become the next great stadium band. The media agreed, with *NME* – who were fast becoming the band's champions – saying, "'Shiver' stamps out their ambitious intent and marks them out as future stars." The single was also helpfully listed on *NME*'s 'Turn Ons' chart at number one for weeks. The record also enjoyed strong exposure on MTV and spots on several B-play lists at prominent radio stations.

To this day, 'Shiver' remains a live favourite, particularly when the crowd invariably attempt to follow Chris's trademark falsetto vocals, usually with ear-shattering results. It is in the live arena that the song's subtleties explode into a wonderful, anthemic, even devotional masterpiece.

Disappointingly, 'Shiver' rose no higher than number 35 in the UK singles charts, but this modest achievement was a relief to Parlophone, which was already anxious to simply get more product out after the numerous false starts in the recording studio. However, it is important to remember that at this stage in Coldplay's career, there had been no 'Yellow', there was no album and their touring experience was limited to shows at smaller-scale venues or as part of a multiple bill. "When 'Shiver' entered the Top 40," admits Will, "it was a real buzz. It was a great surprise and a great thrill."

In May, Coldplay made their television début on *Later ... With Jools Holland*, performing 'Shiver' and a beautiful new song called 'Yellow' that made an immediate impact on the studio audience. The opening chart success of 'Shiver' was then complemented by yet more tour dates, playing alongside Terris and (briefly) Muse. The band openly praised both Muse and another support act, My Vitriol, reinforcing rumours that Coldplay were very 'nice'. (Some members of My Vitriol attended UCL at exactly the same time and in the same year as Coldplay.)

Then it was back on the road for their own headline jaunt, opening at the Leeds Cockpit. This set of gigs was the band's first tour to actually make some money, not least because all but one of the dates were sold out. Despite this growing success, Coldplay's modesty was still very much in evidence. At a gig in Harlow, shortly after the singles chart début, Chris announced 'Shiver' thus: "This was our only ever hit single and it wasn't really much of a hit."

With the chart success of 'Shiver' under their belts, the band was in euphoric mood and so headed back into the studio to continue work on their first long player. The band felt 'Shiver' was the perfect taster to the forthcoming début album: "The general theme of the album and the message we're trying to get across is one of optimism and determination and it's almost like a mirror of our situation; we're on the bottom rung of a very big ladder…"

Before the album could be released, Coldplay had much more to do – not least another relentless round of gigs. Most impressive of all was a second appearance at the Glastonbury Festival, in June 2000. This time around, the festival was being televised on Channel 4, so the pressure was on every band that was performing.

The weekend was a particular triumph for Travis (more of which later). Originally Oasis had been pencilled in to headline Glastonbury but when that failed to happen, Travis stepped into the breach. It was poignant for Coldplay that a band with whom they would so often be compared was doing so well on the main stage.

As for their own performance, the normally humble Coldplay were moved to acknowledge their potential themselves. Despite their mid-afternoon slot and the fact they were on the second (not main) stage, the crowd in the cavernous tent still exceeded 10,000 people. At one point during the set, Chris moved to the mike and said, "Thanks for coming to see us… before we get really Bon Jovi-massive." He later justified this by saying, "It's cos everyone has a go at us for being all humble and everything, I thought it was about time we took the reins."

Noted journalist John Robinson was at the gig and simply said the band, "play one excellent song after another, effortlessly growing in stature. As 'Yellow' captures the crowd's attention, the conclusion 'next year's Travis' is impossible not to reach." Coldplay were equally taken with the experience. "Glastonbury was the best day of the year for us," recounted Chris. "It was the best day of the year for me anyway, I love it."

After each Glastonbury Festival, Michael Eavis organises The Pilton Village Fête, an unadvertised annual gesture to appease local residents weary of the annual invasion of 150,000 mud-caked festival-goers. Bands invited to this one-night 'mini-Glastonbury' frequently go on to headline the main festival at a later date. When Coldplay were asked to play the fête, they agreed immediately. Even though this was a 'small-scale' show, the audience was still over 3,000 people.

After two earlier acts, a voice came through the PA saying, "The guitarist has been taken ill and Coldplay will not be able to perform... Do you want them to perform?" Then on bounded Chris, alone. In keeping with the stripped-down nature of the show, Chris played his first truly solo gig. Sadly, Jon had been diagnosed with glandular fever and so couldn't make it.

Chris was noticeably nervous and muttered a few typically self-deprecating lines in the direction of the crowd: "If you want me to stay, I'll stay, if you want me to go, I'll fuck off." Opening with 'Shiver', he quickly enthralled the crowd. In fact, this show was a fine example of just how versatile his vocals are. Across the eight-song set, he performed countless acrobatics without ever falling into the fatal Christina Aguilera/ Mariah Carey trap of acrobatic self-indulgence. At moments when Jon would normally have pierced the tent's roof with his searing guitars, Chris belted out seemingly impossible falsettos; other times he sat back and let the crowd sing the chorus for him. The nervous tension that lay behind his opening quip faded within minutes and he was soon waltzing around the stage, truly in his element. Coldplay fanatics at the back of the tent who have followed the band since their early days still cite this as being possibly the best gig they have ever seen.

As if the Glasto triumph wasn't enough, the band repeated the performance at an absurdly early 3pm slot at Scotland's T In The Park. This was an unexpected bonus for Coldplay, who were extremely weary from touring Europe and had only arrived from the south of France the night before after a 24-hour bus journey. Their live set here won even more critical acclaim than the Glastonbury show.

The band said they actually enjoyed the day at T In The Park more, mainly because it was not as chaotic. "That was just mental. I'll never forget that," enthused a newly shaven-headed Chris. Neither will indie DJ Steve Lamacq, who was spotted by one reporter reduced to tears by their set. After their show they played an impromptu game of five-a-side football with Embrace that ended in a draw, the last time that the latter band were to be on a par with Coldplay!

Another live highlight of 2000 was Coldplay's show at The Scala in Kings Cross, central London. Although they played only eight songs, the encore was the memorable – albeit rather odd – cover of the Bond theme, 'You Only Live Twice'. Throughout the set, Chris kept repeatedly thanking the crowd for coming, although most of the audience were delighted to see the band in such an intimate venue for what was surely the last time.

A brief flurry around Japan before a similarly received show on the MTV stage at V2000 further bolstered both the band's confidence and their rising profile (at this show Chris said, "The charts don't mean shit to us. But it does feel good to beat The Corrs."). This was also the first time Coldplay spotted a band banner and T-shirt in the crowd, something they all cite as a watershed moment.

With such a bandwagon of festival shows organised and with the exploding profile of the band rising ever higher, it came as a surprise to many that they did not play the double-header Leeds/Reading weekender. Coldplay had a typically banal yet endearing excuse – Chris's father has a cricket team that meets up once a year and as he had missed the event the previous year, he couldn't let his father down again.

CHAPTER 5

Yellow

Although 'Shiver' had given Coldplay their début Top 40 single, 'Yellow' changed *everything*.

The track had its genesis one night at Rockfield. It was a beautiful evening with a panorama of stars easily visible. The members of the band were all outside, looking skywards and generally feeling inspired when the main melody sprang into Chris's head. It didn't seem serious at first, as he relayed the tune to the rest of the band in his worst Neil Young voice. "The song had the word 'stars' and that seemed like a word you should sing in a Neil Young voice."

It wasn't long before Chris had the tempo of the verse worked out, but rather like Paul McCartney using 'scrambled eggs' for the creation of 'Yesterday', he couldn't quite find the right words. He was certain the song needed one *specific* word for its concept and saw 'yellow' written down somewhere in the studio. The lyrics quickly evolved from there, and with Guy, Jon and Will falling enthusiastically into line, they recorded it through the night. They mixed it in New York, although Chris later felt that the vocals were too subdued, too quiet. He later called 'Yellow' a "Welsh song" in deference to the studio where it was conceived.

'Yellow' exemplifies so much of what has made Coldplay so popular. It has a rare and delicate resonance and is shimmeringly beautiful. The opening acoustic guitar chords are mimicked by an electric strumming before plunging into the clanging lead guitar line (strongly reminiscent of Johnny Greenwood from Radiohead), then back into the acoustic verse. Each time the song slows to a stutter before plunging back into the lazy melodies of the verse, it ignites the listener's interest once more.

The luxurious warmth of the instrumentation is underpinned by an ultra-simple drum track, at times as forward in the mix as Chris's vocal, which alters very little throughout verse-to-chorus and contains only a bare minimum of cymbals plus the occasional open hi-hat; likewise the plodding, smooth and occasionally ascending bass. Add to that combination Chris's agile vocal, all wavering emotion, gentle falsetto and near spoken-word whispers (admittedly at its most Jeff Buckley-esque). The Coldplay frontman is never acrobatic with his vocals for the sake of it. The resultant song is a simple yet deeply sophisticated classic.

Of course, with Coldplay nothing is ever as simple as it seems. Famed for their altered tunings, sitting down with a guitar and trying to copy Coldplay chords will leave you with but a dull, busker-like imitation. For example, it was apparent to most muso heads that Chris had detuned his top string to a D sharp, but what was not so apparent was that he also detunes the fourth string down to B (to make it easier to get his fingers round playing the chords). Without such detuning, you can only emulate the sound closely, but never exactly.

The characteristic 'jangle' of the propulsive guitars is a result of similar experimentation. By detuning as described, Chris was able to strum the guitar and leave the top strings ringing out, thus creating that unique, lush sound. This works for the acoustic opening guitar but is also used by Jon for his electric. But then, just when you think you have figured out his nuances, he changes it just a little later on in the song. Yet Jon plays his electric lead line through a conventionally tuned six string. With his deft string-bending, and the clash with the detuned guitar, the resulting surging overdriven guitars moved many enthusiasts to cite classic Sonic Youth. It is exactly this sort of unconventional tuning mixed with radical yet subtle writing that separates Coldplay from the mass of guitar bands out there. Rock 'n' roll they might not be, but bland their songs certainly aren't.

"'Yellow' refers to the mood of the band," explained the singer. "Brightness and hope and devotion. It's quite concise – you don't have to expand on it. It strikes a chord." The fact that stars do not burn yellow, and that many of the things in the song are not yellow either matters little. The references to swimming, bleeding himself dry and drawing a line under something are all metaphorical slants on the extent of Chris's emotional devotion. The reference to drawing a line is a nod to his habit of making lists, and particularly of underlining the most important things on that list. There is even mention of a song-within-a-song, written for the unobtainable object of his affections, a neat self-referential swipe also used by R.E.M. and Idlewild.

Most people actually misread the song as a happy tune with an upbeat theme, even though it was actually another somewhat haunting ode to unrequited love. Chris was single at the time of writing it. Hence the repeated use of the word 'yellow'. "This is a perfect example of [a word] that just sounded good… It just works. I tried not saying that word so much and it didn't sound good. It has a nice ring to it… I don't even like the colour yellow that much… but I was not thinking about the colour as much as something shining like gold."

As for the oddly articulated lyrical themes, he continued in *NME*: "That song is about devotion. That's just about somebody throwing themselves in front of a car for somebody else… if it was your wife or something, or your best mate, I'd do anything for them and they'd do anything for me… The lyrics just arrived. You've gotta have overstatement in your songs, haven't you? I'm sure Atomic Kitten don't really want you to 'do it to them right now', but that's how it comes across."

The video for the single was conceived and produced entirely by the band. Initially, the concept was for all four members to be walking along a beach, bathed in sunshine, keeping things simple and bright. However, the actual shoot fell on the same day as Will's mother's funeral, so Chris was alone when they rolled up to record the footage. This might go some way to explaining the genuinely sombre mood Chris seems to be in during this clip.

The weather was atrocious and the rain unrelenting. Ever the pragmatist, it was decided to record the footage in the minimum amount of time possible – 20 minutes – and go home for a warm bath. Thus was created the famous minimal footage of Chris walking on the sands, bracing himself against the wind and rain. It could not have been more fitting and MTV and the countless other music channels that had recently sprung up through the growth of digital TV placed the clip on immediate heavy rotation.

This TV exposure for 'Yellow' was matched by a tidal wave of radio play, particularly at BBC Radio 1, where Lamacq again championed the single. For the first time, hard-to-please regional stations classed the track as completely radio-friendly and consequently started to pick up on Coldplay too. Even the newly revitalised BBC Radio 2 played the track repeatedly. This airplay continued for weeks, indeed months, after the track was released, eventually making 'Yellow' Y2K's most aired radio tune.

NME – regularly derided for being wide of the mark in predicting success for also-rans – spotted a legend in the making. The undertone of its review for 'Yellow' suggested it had wanted to deliver a harsh, negative appraisal, but just couldn't: "Coldplay are the Sunday School kids brought in to provide a little heart-warming interdenominational harmony. It's amazing how they get away with this. There's something undeniably enchanting about them. Whatever moves 'Yellow' beyond the realm of drippy 'Thom-Buckley' pastiche, it's a true gift."

'Yellow' was released in June 2000, the same week the band played their first continental dates. They were in the Netherlands when they heard the stunning news that the song's midweek sales suggested it would go in the Top 10. At that point, they all agreed that even if it slipped back into the Top 20 it would still be a triumph, and either way a huge progression from the number 35 enjoyed by 'Shiver'. As it was, 'Yellow' enjoyed stronger sales in the second half of the week and finally charted at a lofty number four.

That night they were actually playing a gig in Holland to a very small audience of people who had never heard of Coldplay. After the show, Phil Harvey walked into the dressing room (such as it was) and told them the news. The band were shocked.

Coldplay were invited on to (the now-defunct) *Top of the Pops*, a traditional rite of passage for all bands hoping to prove to their doubting aunts and uncles that pop music was a worthwhile career. Better still, their dressing room was opposite that of Victoria Beckham and her England football captain husband David. Now, surely, Coldplay were a *proper* band.

'Yellow' was not just the anthem of the summer in the UK. The song went around the world and almost overnight Coldplay were the band on the tips of everyone's tongues. "I think we got really super caught-up in how amazingly huge it was," recalls Jon, "and it was like, 'Wow, all these people are singing our song.'" Will remains perplexed as to the extent of the success of 'Yellow': "I don't know what it is about that song that made it so huge. If we knew what it was about that song that made it so popular, [our] next album would be the biggest-selling album of all time." Within six months of its original release, there was even a Chinese pop star covering the song.

As it was, 'Yellow' turned Coldplay into very serious contenders on the rock scene and in the process sold millions of copies worldwide. It also earned them a clutch of award nominations and actual trophies including: *Q* Awards 'Best Single'; second place for *NME* 'Single Of The Year'; 'Single Of The Year' in *Select* magazine; 'Best Single' and 'Best Video' nominations at the Brit Awards; and *NME* Brat Awards 'Best Single'.

More importantly, the single was crucial in the public perception of Coldplay. If *The Joshua Tree* was U2's turning point, then 'Yellow' was a mini-version of the same for Coldplay. Now universally acknowledged as a classic ballad, the song has since gone on to receive some of the most generous plaudits. Fellow songwriters and artists were quick to heap praise on the track and Coldplay. Elton John said 'Yellow' was "the only song from the last five years that I wish I had written". Puff Daddy and Justin Timberlake were other stars who fell over themselves to praise the song. Liam Gallagher came backstage after a later Coldplay show at the Shepherd's Bush Empire in west London and told Chris that the song, "made him want to start writing songs again". He subsequently wrote 'Songbird', a tribute to his new wife and ex-All Saints star, Nicole

Appleton, a single that later went Top 3. Liam even leant over to Chris and sang the song in his ear.

For some more reluctant supporters, 'Yellow' was proof positive that Coldplay were – as previously suggested – the new Travis. Not Radiohead or U2, but Travis. In 1999, the Scottish pop melodists had seemingly come from nowhere to claim all the honours, with a clutch of brilliant opening singles, peaking with the tender 'Driftwood' and the anthemic 'Why Does It Always Rain On Me?' Their frontman, Fran Healy, quickly became the alternative pin-up of choice, while their album, *The Man Who*, hit the top spot and sold multi-platinum. Relentless touring and close camaraderie were just two more examples of similarities between Coldplay and Travis, so it was clear why the 'new Travis' comments would not go away.

While such comparisons are entertaining over a drink and provide endless copy for magazines, they can in fact be very damaging to a band's career. Embrace were tagged as the next Oasis, but they never seemed able to climb out from under that suffocating label. It has cost many bands dearly. For Coldplay, it was vital that the comparisons with Travis (and Radiohead), however flattering, were not allowed to spiral out of control. They would often joke about the comparisons, but were also not averse to acknowledging them: fast-forward to 2007 and Chris would début Travis' new single on Radio 1 by saying, "We're gonna finish with an incredible exclusive, we're very privileged to play it, it's a new song by the band Travis, the band that invented my band and lots of others." The only way to prevent continued musical comparisons causing lasting damage was to deliver songs that identified Coldplay as very much their own men.

Another approach was to self-eulogise. At a show in Norwich several months after 'Yellow' charted, Chris introduced 'Yellow' like this: "In the Seventies, there was Queen's 'Bohemian Rhapsody', in the Eighties there was Duran Duran's 'Rio' and in the Nineties 'Runaway Train' by Soul Asylum. We're Coldplay and this is 'Yellow'." He later reflected on this and refused to back down, saying, "What I was trying to say there was that I do think it's a really important song, perhaps even a defining one."

More poignantly, however, such tongue-in-cheek comments were never going to be as important as their actual recorded output in putting these positive but ultimately unhelpful comparisons to rest. Fortunately, with the forthcoming début album set for a July 2000 release, Coldplay were about to silence all the doubters and detractors in one fell swoop.

CHAPTER 6

One Thousand, Two Thousand, Three Thousand... Check... Five Million

Initially, Coldplay had intended to record their first album in a brief two-week spell. This was highly idealistic of course, not least because it took no account whatsoever of their sometimes fierce tendency to pursue perfectionism or their previous slow track record in the studio. As it turned out, the album was eventually recorded in bursts between tours and sporadic live dates from September 1999 and April/May 2000. Consequently, several studios were used, including the by-now familiar Rockfield, plus Parr Street in Liverpool and Matrix and Wessex Studios in London (apart from the mellow 'High Speed', which was recorded at Orinoco Studios with Chris Allison).

Coldplay admitted that at times the multitude of sessions were pretty awful. Weeks of smashing things, rowing and ego-driven strops might make people who regarded them as 'nice boys' think about this supposed genteel band somewhat differently, they suggested.

At the production helm was Ken Nelson, who had previously worked with Gomez and Badly Drawn Boy. He worked alongside Mark

Phythain, who programmed the computers. The standard Coldplay set-up was complemented by a pair of Fender Twins and a Jaguar guitar for Jon (previously he had been a Telecaster die-hard). Chris purchased an old Jazzmaster too, which Jon would often use, although the faithful Telecaster still appears on the majority of the songs.

The material that was written fresh for the album usually followed the Coldplay routine of Chris bringing a melody or sequence of chords to the rest of the band, who then put their own stamp on it. "It's like a factory production line," explained Will. "It just moves on to the next stage and it's not over until all of us have done our bit. And all our bits have to be agreed on by everyone else." Despite being so obviously central to the band's success, Chris has never claimed to be a solo singer-songwriter and enjoys the musical tensions and debates that being in a band creates. During an internet Q&A with fans, he also distanced himself from the purely autobiographical school of writing, instead suggesting that, "Songwriting is a mix of fiction and myth. Things are very romanticised. A song is like a film in that you can say anything you want. So there are parts that are based on truth and there are also parts that just sound good or feel good. It's a mixture of the two. It's all imagery. It's not strictly truth."

Similar to the pressure they felt when recording their first major label EP with Chris Alison, the band found the tension of delivering their first album quite suffocating too and there were rumours of arguments and uncertainty creeping into the foursome again. However, they eventually pulled through and completed the record a week before mixing began. "In terms of music," recalled Chris, "it was the hardest thing we've ever had to do, and in terms of friendship and our commitment. It was more a case of frustration… the most important thing is that every song, we've really got a feeling into it. And that's the first priority."

They toyed with several names for the album, including *Don't Panic*, *Yellow* and *Help Is Round The Corner* before settling on *Parachutes*. Again there was a metaphorical reason, essentially that the thrust of the record was about how certain things in life can seem like they are destined to end in failure or tragedy, but that there was often a safety net, a parachute, which plucked you back from the brink. For the UK's supposed premier miserabilists, this was veritable optimism. The album cover – photographed by the band themselves – was a shot of the illuminated globe of planet Earth, which they took on the road with them, usually seen perched atop Chris's keyboards or nearby on an amplifier.

When asked whether they expected a high chart placing for the record, they were understandably reticent to commit: "If we've learned anything from how 'Yellow' did then it's that you can't predict anything."

In the weeks prior to the album's release, the band had an intense and exciting strategy of promotional work planned. Yet they were already counselling themselves in the event that the album was panned. In terms of the record itself, they remained calmly hopeful about its prospects: "We just set out to make an emotional, passionate record, with good songs obviously. We were pleased with it, but it's always hard when you've finished something like that, to know if it's any good or not."

The very least you can say about *Parachutes* is that it is "good". One of the finest and most understated début albums of recent times, the record instantly transformed Coldplay from "the new Travis" into a group who would quickly far surpass the achievements of that Scottish outfit. Bearing in mind that the band were barely into their twenties, this was a record of rare accomplishment, subtlety and sophistication, displaying a maturity well beyond their years.

The album's new material is reinforced by their three EMI/Parlophone singles, 'Shiver', 'Yellow' and two tracks from *The Blue Room EP*, 'High Speed' and 'Don't Panic'. In all, only ten tracks, but this was sheer quality, not quantity.

The opening track, 'Don't Panic', was in many ways a perfect indication of what was to follow. A notably short song, it begins with Chris's soft acoustic strumming, followed shortly after by Jon's piercing guitar lines, segued with an imploring vocal. This was an opening song that immediately made you sit up and take notice. When taken in the context of the then-in-vogue (and initially brilliant) nu-metal noise, this was a clear, refreshingly brief and charming statement of melancholic intent. The lyrical lead of living in a beautiful world again defies the accusations of miserabilism and sets the album off in the perfect manner.

Next up was the aforementioned Parlophone single 'Shiver', which raised the tempo somewhat, with its *OK Computer* drums and spidery guitars. This track typifies the simple sentiments of so much of *Parachutes*, often touching on themes and emotions that everyone experiences. Then it is straight into the album's most atmospheric track, the wistful and delightful 'Spies'. Débuted at the Reading Festival in 1999, this song's acoustic refrains are both foreboding and sumptuous, while the lead guitar picks are contrasted nicely by the Larry Mullen Jr-esque falling drum lines; but this was no U2 pastiche. By now, the textures and depth of Chris's vocals were really settling into the listener's psyche and this is a clear stand-out track. His falsetto pitches against the rising momentum and building rhythm beautifully, a clashing mix of jagged guitars and simple vocal balladry. Then the band drop the dynamics right back down, refusing to head-rush for the obvious thunderous climax, instead winding the song down to just the gentle repeated vocal line over a feather-soft acoustic wash. (Bizarrely, this song was later banned by an overly censurous Chinese government for alleged "unacceptable political connotations".)

Refusing to up the tempo, the fourth track is the even softer 'Sparks'. Jeff Buckley and perhaps Nick Drake are the obvious reference points, but once more this is no mere tribute song. Chris's voice crumbles at times, before soaring into the gently controlled heights that he seems to be able to reach effortlessly.

Smack bang in the middle of the album is the clear masterpiece, 'Yellow'. Even if this had, as some feared, been the only decent track on the album, it would not have mattered. More than any other song, this will always be their signal of intent, a notice of ambition, their manifesto, their totem. With this single piece of music, they will always justifiably be held up as classic songwriters.

Future single 'Trouble' achieves the impossible and follows one of the greatest songs of recent times without appearing feeble by comparison. The soon-to-be world famous piano tinkerings at the song's opening confirm that here is a band unafraid to swim against the tide of fashion. When all around were using distorted guitars, onstage DJs and infinite Marshall stacks, here was a delicately crafted song that sounded quite exquisite, whether played solo by Chris at his piano or more emphatically by the entire band.

Again Chris uses the lyrical trick of repetition, centring on the word trouble, although unlike 'Yellow' with more obvious reason. This is one of the few Coldplay songs that Chris has opened up about, suggesting that 'Trouble' was the result of his own bad behaviour: "There were some bad things going on in our band… the song is about behaving badly towards somebody you really love and I was certainly doing that to some members of the band. I suppose it's about a time when I was being a bit of a knobhead." Of course, how he phrases that crude regret in musical terms is poignant, emotional and pure.

Once again the apparently minimalist sound belies the ingenious production process. The multiple snare rattles are mixed very low behind the desolate lead piano, so as to be almost inaudible by the time Jon's ringing guitars crash in. Yet there they are, keeping the momentum rolling, splicing each verse and chorus together seamlessly; a perfect example of "less is more". Critics might have started lambasting the softer emotional themes, the apologies, the unrequited love, the longing, but set against such a backdrop of gentle musical texture, this was hardly ever going to be an album for metalheads.

The album's title track clocks in at just over 40 seconds, somewhat disappointing when you hear the melody. Produced with a minimum of effects and unobtrusive ambience, the skin scraping up the guitar strings is not only audible, but actively part of the song. Why they chose to truncate such a promising tune to a virtual still-birth has never been explained, but it is a shame. Maybe it never evolved into a fuller song, or maybe this was the exact intention, to leave the listener craving more. Nonetheless, 'Parachutes' is the first sign on the album of the understated slipping towards being almost nonexistent.

Weakest track on the album is the rather weedy 'High Speed'. Sounding like Travis at their wimpiest, the song never really takes off. Although Chris's vocals are compelling and the lyrics deftly arranged, the momentum doesn't quite build up. Elements of the drums and bass sound recognisable but are actually rather derivative of earlier tracks. Fortunately this track gains strength on stage but on the album the dynamics seem too weak, promising potential but never fully evolving, even though early producer Chris Allison had clearly done a sterling job with the material in front of him. Hardly a poor track, for sure, but in such esteemed company, there was little room for error.

The penultimate track, 'We Never Change', kicks back the tempo and volume but returns the album to its lofty standards. Again opening with yet another acoustic refrain underneath Chris's accomplished voice, the song saunters along until Jon's piercing string-bending and almost Shadows-like solitary note-picking lift the chorus into the stars. At first, the piano is barely touched, almost brushed across a few keys, while the bass simply follows the root note, without pretension but with great self-control (although elsewhere Guy's jazz influences are plain to hear). Even the rising climax contains fewer notes and less sound than most band's studio tune-ups. At times, Chris sounds almost as if he is falling asleep while singing, particularly on the final few lines, where a hint of laconic apathy seems to fit perfectly.

Ending on a typically obtuse note, 'Everything's Not Lost' clocks in as the longest song on the album at over seven minutes. One of Chris Martin's particular favourites, this song once more offers piano tickles, guitar riffing of the most subtle and choosy kind, almost spoken-word vocals with fathoms of character and a masterful, polished production. Just like the opening 'Don't Panic' had hinted at the excellence to come, this track reminds us of what had passed and instantly urges us to press the 'repeat' button. Just as you do, a hidden song catches up with you, offering a short, almost fairground waltz apology to a lover. Throughout the track, the drums remind the listener of the superb Flaming Lips, an airy, expansive rhythm backing that Chris admitted was a straight influence after having seen the Lips play a few months previously. Introspective and wonderful.

OK, many of the lyrics were largely incomprehensible. But hey, Thom Yorke had been hailed as a rock deity for singing about unborn chickens. And certainly Oasis were never going to trouble the Booker Prize judging panel. Chris deliberately steers clear of overtly political lyrics – at one stage Coldplay wrote a song that was a scathing attack on the tabloid media, but it was never recorded.

Of course, the influences and comparisons were obvious and multiple: U2, with many hints of the Edge's effects-laden guitar yet simplified infinitely; reminders of why Echo & The Bunnymen were one of the great bands (Jon made no secret of his love of Bunnymen guitarist Will Sergeant); The Verve's Richard Ashcroft and for that matter their guitarist Nick McCabe; the late lamented Boo Radleys, particularly 'Lazarus'; of course Radiohead, almost at every turn glimpses of Yorke and Greenwood; The Flaming Lips; Kevin Shields' My Bloody Valentine; elements of the languorous side of Pink Floyd that made *Dark Side Of The Moon* so appealing; Neil Young… or was it Nick Drake?; the softer edge of Matt Bellamy's Muse even… and so on and so on.

Yet somehow none of this seemed to matter. With the quite remarkable atmospheres of *Parachutes*, the four former students successfully sucked up all their quite open influences and spewed out a uniquely delicate, enveloping warmth via a simply stunning album so ingeniously crafted and expertly delivered that only one band stuck in the mind at the end of the final closing note: Coldplay.

The context of *Parachutes'* release makes it all the more impressive. True, other bands had been tagged miserabilist, such as Doves, Muse, even Travis, but none had released a record like this. At the upper reaches of the commercial charts, the noisy behemoth of nu-metal, which had revitalised the tired metal genre and turned record books upside down in the rock-versus-metal debate, was sadly turning into self-parody, leaving Fred Durst enjoying increasingly less acclaim while suspiciously polished outfits like Linkin Park still sold vast amounts of records (their *Hybrid Theory* was the world's top selling album in 2001).

In the world of pop, reality shows were spewing up the occasional pearl among a morass of wannabes and the charts were filled with diluted trance, sugary pop and predominantly clichéd mainstream rap. Meanwhile, the all-conquering post-*OK Computer* Radiohead were about to veer off deeply into the experimental realms of the abrasive *Kid A*; Oasis were telling everyone who would listen that their *Be Here Now* album disappointed even them; Blur were heading for an unseemly part-split while the dance ubermeisters Prodigy remained on a lengthy sabbatical after their gruelling world tour for the 10 million-selling *The Fat Of The Land* album; hip hop was still struggling to pull its core genius away from the clichéd and repetitive; Stereophonics and Travis had sneaked into the gap to take the crown of British rock but here, suddenly, was a very serious new contender. In time, The Strokes would arrive and drastically shake up the music world, complemented by the eventual launch overground of UK garage, but for now Coldplay were head and shoulders above the competition.

Given this environment of predominantly nu-metal and pop, the fact that Coldplay had chosen to make their début in such a stripped back, naked style, that they were all only just out of their teens, and that they had been together for only 32 months made *Parachutes* an even more astounding achievement.

CHAPTER 7

(Un)fitter, But Happier?

An intense period of promotion was planned for the days leading up to the release of *Parachutes*. Radio coverage was again substantial – Steve Lamacq's *Evening Session* continued its championing of the band by featuring several of the tracks. More prominently, the band played an in-store gig at the enormous HMV record store in London's Oxford Street. Over 700 fans, music press and Coldplay friends and associates crammed into the venue (there was a *very* limited amount of tickets on the door on the night) for a short, live performance featuring 'Spies', 'Don't Panic', 'Bigger, Stronger', 'Trouble', 'Yellow' and 'Everything's Not Lost', after which they signed copies of the album. The event was webcast and broadcast on Xfm.

"We do a lot of these but it was one of the best I've ever seen," Simon Winter, HMV's spokesman, told *NME*.com. "We were absolutely up to our limit capacity-wise, and I had to turn fans away outside. Almost everybody there last night bought a copy of the album and sales today indicate they could be number one by a long shot."

Winter was not wrong. The combination of anticipation, the sheer quality of the record and clever promotion meant that on the Monday of release, over 20,000 people were moved to go out and buy it. By the end of the week another 40,000 copies had been shifted, easily sending

Parachutes to the top of the album charts. Dan Keeling at Parlophone had set a *total* sales target of 40,000, a figure that reflected the relatively modest investment in modern record-deal terms.

These sales were moderately impressive, albeit way short of the hundreds of thousands often sold by the world's top acts. Oasis and Radiohead at their peak would have sold several hundred thousand copies in their first week. Coldplay, however, had legs and over the coming months the record hovered in or around the edges of the Top 10 until Christmas. In the process sales in the UK rose to more than 1.6 million, in other words, in excess of *five times platinum*.

There were several reasons why *Parachutes* enjoyed such longevity and accelerating sales. Firstly, the media almost universally hailed the record as a masterpiece. Few bands could dream of reviews like these. *NME*: "(Chris) has poured every thought, every feeling he's had in the last two years into this record… it's like reading one long, intimate love letter. Some moments here indicate there's more to him than anyone knows. 9/10"; Q magazine: "You can only wonder what well of emotional trauma has been dredged for some of what's on offer here. Halls of residence will echo with this record for months to come, but the rest of the world could do worse than listen. 4/5"; *Uncut:* "A sensational opening gambit and one that more than justifies the plaudits heaped upon them by the weekly music press. A wonderful record, very special indeed. 4/5"; *Melody Maker:* "Album of the Year! It's a fucking masterpiece!" and "very likely a defining musical statement of 2000".

It was actually difficult to find a bad review. Indeed, one of the few critical pieces written was actually a retrospective look at the album while reviewing Coldplay's follow-up record in 2002. It came from *The Guardian's* Alexis Petridis who said *Parachutes* was "certainly no masterpiece. So timid it sounded like it was apologising for bothering you, its wan balladry was enough to make you wonder how rock music became so beige."

The second factor behind those colossal home sales was the success of the next single, 'Trouble', which went Top 10. This reflected the band's higher profile, not least because the album with this song on was already out. Later, UK trance outfit Lost Witness remixed 'Trouble', a release that became an unlikely dance-floor anthem. Initially, the plan was to release

'Don't Panic' from *Parachutes* as well, but in the end the band decided that just the three singles was enough from that one record in the UK; in Europe 'Don't Panic' was put out as a single though.

Although three singles from an album was quite conservative by their peers' standards, when coupled with the seemingly endless airplay for previous singles, in particular 'Yellow', this ensured that Coldplay were rarely off the UK's airwaves, even when they were touring tirelessly abroad.

A third key element of the album's success was the string of awards it garnered, even though the absurd proliferation of modern-day rock and pop award ceremonies has served only to dilute the impact and importance of many of these prizes. Nonetheless, despite the rather clichéd insistence of so many bands – most famously Gorillaz – that awards are totally irrelevant, such ceremonies still matter. They are often televised and watched by non-committed music fans who rarely listen to the radio and probably buy less than 10 albums a year, and these consumers are invariably influenced by consistent exposure at awards ceremonies.

By the time *Parachutes* was heading towards the million mark in December, the media were already preparing copies of their end of year 'Best Of…' listings. Thus the Coldplay album easily won the 'Best Album Of 2000' plaudits handed out by *Select* and *Q* magazine, while they managed a slightly more disappointing Top 10 placing in *NME's* list.

When *NME* chose its anti-establishment Brat Awards after the New Year, Coldplay came home winners again. More importantly, they were nominated for several Brit Awards, including 'Best British Group', 'Best Album', 'Best Single' and 'Best Video' for 'Yellow'. On winning the first two, Chris was clearly taken aback: "Shit, shit, shit. This is the weirdest thing that ever happened to us. All around us are bands we used to listen to when we were at school, sitting eating their tea. It's weird, and it's great. Thanks very much."

Later, when he returned to collect the 'Best Album' gong, he recounted a time when he was supposed to be playing cricket at school but had also booked a gig that would prevent him from doing both. He said his teacher suggested that as he was useless at cricket he should play the show. "If we hadn't have done that, I'd probably be playing for Essex or something now. Thank you to him for making us what we are."

By December of 2000 *Parachutes* did indeed pass the one million copies mark in the UK – only 960,000 more than the record company target.

The fourth factor in building these stunning sales figures – and the band's growing critical reputation – was the continued heavy touring that Simon Williams had highlighted as a long-standing part of the band's psyche. Just prior to the album's launch, they played a homecoming gig for Chris at Exeter's Cavern Club and the crowd reaction was an indication of what was about to happen to Coldplay in the coming months.

Chris was visibly thrilled to be playing Exeter and asked the audience to all say hello to his parents who were in attendance. "This is great! It's what you dream of at school!" Unfortunately, *NME*'s Victoria Segal was less than impressed: "There's something undeniably irritating about a band who try quite so hard to be ordinary, who would rather offer up the drippy piano apologies of 'Trouble' than face up to a hammer-and-tongs fight, who tell the audience with such merry shrugging 'we haven't got all the answers', when the best bands have you believing they have a smudged copy of *The Book Of Life* under their beds." However, Segal was in a tiny minority if Coldplay ticket sales were anything to go by. That autumn, the band embarked on their first large-scale UK headlining tour, which sold out within hours.

While the plaudits continued to pour in for Coldplay's album and live show, Chris was predictably more self-deprecating. He has even admitted that he impersonates Bono at home and ended up using elements of this mimicry on stage, particularly the heavy breathing and crackled vocals that the U2 man so often delivers. Chris's notorious one-liners and ad-libbing in between songs has led to more comparisons with Thom Yorke, although Chris feels his conversational style is still littered with inappropriate comments: "Nine out of ten times I come off stage and say, 'That was a good gig, but I'm sorry for being such a knob.'" In Portsmouth for one show, the band had to agree, not least because Chris walked out and said, "Hello Plymouth!"

Among this legion of dates were several shows that proved central to the band's success. An acoustic-only gig – the band's first – at Ronnie Scott's in Birmingham on July 30 was an enjoyable precursor to a lengthy series of home dates. Though they had previously given unplugged radio performances of 'Yellow' and 'Shiver' in particular, this was the first full set before such a demanding and musically educated audience.

Complementing these smaller shows were some highly successful appearances at major festivals, most notably at the V2000 Festival in Chelmsford and Staffordshire. The larger shows blended with smaller-scale gigs and more private affairs: in August, they taped an afternoon set at the tiny Monarch pub in north London's Camden, recorded for the forthcoming TV series *The Barfly Sessions*, which was to be aired on Channel 4.

Many of these smaller shows were already booked before *Parachutes* had been released, so the lucky few who booked tickets for gigs at venues such as Edinburgh Liquid Rooms and Portsmouth Pyramids could see a band that, next time around, would surely be playing huge arenas. The London date on this autumn 2000 UK tour was merely a single show at the Shepherd's Bush Empire. Some sold-out venues displayed signs saying disappointed fans were welcome to sit outside and listen to whatever they could make out.

Barely pausing for breath, Coldplay headed out to Italy for two festivals (where they told native journalists how much they enjoyed playing on the same bill as Marlene Kuntz), before returning to the UK for a BBC session, then back out two days later for a show in Barcelona, then back to the UK for two more shows that week before flying out to Japan within four days for the Summer Sonic Festival, before a two-week gap leading to first the Bizarre Festival in Cologne, Germany and straight home for V2000! With the road crew having barely finished packing up the gear, they had to reopen the flight cases at a festival in Holland and then at another in Belgium.

This blitz across Europe mixed actual shows with heavy album promotion and a smattering of acoustic gigs, in-store signings and radio sessions. Prior to the album's release, Coldplay had played about 100 gigs in total, so such an extensive international campaign was quite a culture shock. Within five weeks they pretty much travelled to most corners of western Europe, cramming dozens of interviews into each day before playing a show most nights. As if in an effort to clock up air miles, among this continental trek were three dates in the southern hemisphere, at Auckland, Melbourne and Sydney.

After a superb 'secret' show at the tiny Kentish Town Bull & Gate – where in a sense it had all started – for Coldplay's own Christmas celebration at the end of an incredible year, they enjoyed a few precious days off before the treadmill started all over again. The relentless pace picked up with another day-long flight to New Zealand and Australia for dates around that subcontinent before flying across the Pacific to begin a North American campaign.

Ideally, they would have wanted the promo tours for *Parachutes* to be over by Christmas. In reality they were only just starting. On the surface, Coldplay were coping well but the high-energy performances gave no hint of the cracks that were emerging.

Coldplay in Chicago on November 30, 2001. (NATKIN/WIREIMAGE)

"This is not what we meant about 'Going down The Ivy.'" Left to right: Guy Berryman, Will Champion, Chris Martin and Jonny Buckland. (MICK HUTSON/REDFERNS)

Classic Chris Martin on stage. (DENNIS VAN TINE/LFI UDV)

At The Millennium Dome, London, September 26, 2000. (SIMON MEAKER/LFI)

Young and with the world at their feet, or at least just to their side. (BENEDICT JOHNSON/REDFERNS)

A very young-looking Coldplay wish they'd not been so puritanical with their rider. (BENEDICT JOHNSON/REDFERNS)

At their first Brit Awards, February 28, 2001. (JMENTERNATIONAL/REDFERNS)

You'd never guess that until just recently they were students. (L. COHEN/WIREIMAGE)

Erstwhile bassist and multi-instrumentalist Guy Berryman. (PAUL NATKIN/WIREIMAGE)

Jonny playing his Fender Telecaster Thinline onstage at the KROQ Christmas Special. (CHRISTINA RADISH/REDFERNS)

Who says we play music for bed-wetters? (MICK HUTSON/REDFERNS)

CHAPTER 8

Bed-wetters, Plain And Simple

With the press files spilling over with gushing reviews and the award cabinets sagging under the weight of the gongs they'd captured, it is fair to say that Coldplay had enjoyed almost universal acclaim. Almost.

There were detractors and, unfortunately for the band, this included Alan McGee, one of the music industry's most successful and colourful characters. Owner of Creation Records, McGee signed Oasis and boasted an independent label roster that included, alongside the Mancunian brothers, Primal Scream, Teenage Fanclub and a host of other critically revered acts. So it is fair to say his opinions about music came eminently well qualified.

The stage for McGee to voice his distaste for Coldplay's music was the Mercury Music Prize nominations for 2000. With a history of surprising and often left-field winners, the prize of £25,000 and critical nods were nonetheless much sought after. Coldplay were installed as 3/1 favourites to win, ahead of other nominees including Richard Ashcroft, Leftfield, Death In Vegas, Doves, Badly Drawn Boy and Nitin Sawhney. As it turned out, the winner was 10/1 outsider Badly Drawn Boy, with their album *The Hour Of Bewilderbeast*.

McGee's problem was that he was disgusted at the list of nominees, especially since *Parachutes* had been short-listed when one of his own acts, Primal Scream, hadn't. McGee had always championed his bands passionately but it was the manner in which he chose to articulate his displeasure that took many by surprise.

In a very public display of rancour, McGee vented his fury in a lengthy and brutally direct article in *The Guardian*, deriding Coldplay as "wimps" and "music for bed-wetters". Only a month later, McGee added fuel to the fire when he used an interview in *Melody Maker* to take another swipe at them. Talking about Kurt Cobain's widow, Courtney Love, he said, "She's about real punk rock, she's what it's all about, not like those twats in Coldplay. Coldplay are like something from an ice-cream advert, just complete careerists. They might as well be saying, 'Bend me over the desk and fuck me up the arse.' It's pathetic." So at least it was clear now that McGee wasn't a big fan.

This was sensational stuff for the music press, ever hungry for a headline. Readers either laughed, read into it that British music was dying, or just read it and moved on. Others felt McGee was right to demand more rock 'n' roll excess; opponents suggested he seemed to have hastily forgotten some of the output of his own label, such as the Eighties band Biff Bang Pow!, whose songs included 'If You Don't Love Me Now You Never Ever Will' and 'Hug Me Honey'. And his label's "critics' favourites", Teenage Fanclub, could hardly be said to be competing with Motley Crüe for the title of the 'World's Most Outrageous Band'.

Others suggested that McGee, ever the opportunist, was cynically grabbing headlines to promote his own label. Creation had released the controversial new solo album by former Dexy's Midnight Runners frontman Kevin Rowland, which suffered a public mauling both for the music and the much-derided pseudo-transvestite imagery that Rowland displayed in his live shows. Rumours suggested that despite a substantial PR campaign from Creation, the Rowland album sold very poorly, leading many harsh pundits to talk of it as one of the most badly reviewed albums ever released.

Also, to McGee's chagrin, the Oasis bubble appeared to be bursting. The Gallagher brothers had enjoyed a high profile and garnered countless column inches through their explosive personalities, but their "rock stars in mansions with expensive habits" lifestyle of late had for many fans taken the edge off what had actually made them so appealing in the first place. Noel and Liam themselves were, of course, veterans of the band slanging match, having taken media insults to new heights with their relentless pillorying of Blur. By comparison, being called a bed-wetter seemed almost a compliment.

Furthermore, although multi-platinum sales and fatherhood had evidently mellowed the Gallagher brothers, they were their usual quote-friendly-selves when they bumped into Chris backstage at a London show. Liam leant into his ear and said, "Don't worry 'bout fookin' McGee. We like ya. And if McGee doesn't like the new album then we really are shit."

Coldplay's reaction to this tirade from McGee was twofold. In the media, with the press sensing the first whiff of a genuine rock 'n' roll spat for ages, they came out fighting. "[I don't] give a shit what he has to say. It doesn't matter," said an apparently scornful Chris, while Jon said, "We are trying to be who we are, but that's about it. Pretending to be 'a bit mad' would just be sad." Other verbal parries to the McGee thrust were reported to include, "Yes, but he's just an old punk, isn't he?"; "Well, that doesn't concern us in the slightest. It's not even worth responding to, really"; "We don't hit people. I'm tempted to have a go at that bloke who used to run that label but I just can't be bothered. That whole thing about him – I forget his name…"; Jonny provided the most McGee-baiting quote of all: "On balance, I'd take nice over being called a cunt any day." On a more serious note, what bemused Coldplay most of all was that McGee's criticism was directed at them personally and the venom was not the result of any actual feud, since McGee and the band had never met.

In typically diplomatic fashion, Coldplay also made placatory remarks about some of the bands on Creation, suggesting that a man who had signed Teenage Fan Club, Ride and Oasis had a right to an opinion and even went as far as to say that *XTRMNTR* (the Primal Scream album that had missed out on a Mercury Prize nomination, which had so infuriated McGee in the first place), was a great record. So after their initial defensive reaction, they had reacted – publicly at least – to being accused of being too nice by being… nice.

Privately, however, the bitter attack made a deep impact. The success of *Parachutes* had surprised everyone and the band found themselves thrust headlong into a relentless machine of media and promotion. Matters were exacerbated by the fact that their profile in the UK rocketed at a time when they were actually promoting the same album in Europe, so they returned to find, almost without warning, a nation that was suddenly Coldplay crazy.

Cracks started to show. Chris in particular seemed to have taken the recent digs very personally and his uncertainty suggested he was having a difficult time coming to terms with the vitriol that can flow so freely around the music world. "We're starting to feel that everyone's out to get us," he told *Melody Maker*. "The more people that like us, the more people seem to hate us, and it's something nobody tells you how to deal with. A lot of people seem to take it really personally that we're doing well, and I hate that… We're not evil politicians trying to swindle the whole world."

Chris even went as far as to suggest that McGee was ultimately right and that their album did not deserve to win the Mercury Prize because, "it's for trailblazers and we're not trailblazers yet. We constantly see bands we think are better than us." His self-doubt appeared to be rampant.

Worse still, there were industry rumours that the spell in the firing line had caused the band to turn in on itself, with whispers of stress, illness, possible splits and inter-band arguments. The ferocity of the criticism and the depth of the loyalty seemed to have shocked Chris. "People who don't like you talk about you like you're the Third Reich. People who do like you will really defend you. So [at the moment] it's a mixture of extreme excitement and extreme, er, panic."

With the continued success of *Parachutes* creating an ever-increasing spiral of commitments across the globe, it seemed there was a real possibility that Coldplay would implode, crushed by the weight of their own success. The Mercury Music Prize awards ceremony thus seemed like an almost unnecessary final lap after the contest that had been bubbling so fiercely in the media for weeks. Jon was ill and unable to attend so Coldplay performed 'Yellow' as a three-piece. There were no major incidents, no waving of anyone's Oxfam-besuited bottom at Michael Jackson. It all seemed rather superfluous. And besides, they didn't win the Mercury Prize anyway. In his acceptance speech, Badly

Drawn Boy paid generous tribute to Coldplay for being gracious losers and so supportive of his work despite losing out. Nice.

Some months later when the dust had begun to settle and Chris and the rest of the band were in a more philosophical mood, they had clearly managed to draw something positive from McGee's outburst. Chris unashamedly told Q magazine: "You know what? I would like to shake Alan McGee by the hand. Quite right of him to give us a kick up the arse. I say, 'Bring it on', because it makes me think, 'I'll show you'. I don't like feeling inferior to anyone… I don't wanna feel there's a guy out there who's better than me."

CHAPTER 9

Cauliflower-gate

"It's hard work being a soddin' icon 24 hours a day."

Ian McCulloch

In the ocean of weirdness and contradiction that is the music world, still waters do indeed run deep. While the release of *Parachutes* and the subsequent critical adulation, multi-million sales and sold-out tours created the impression that Coldplay were a band on the crest of an incredible wave, underneath the surface things were very different indeed.

Much has been made of Coldplay's rather fragile creative state, and Chris Martin has made no secret of the fact that he often worried himself sick. More often than not, he keeps his anxieties to himself, but there are times when his public behaviour and dialogue with the press seemed to reflect this demeanour. Way back when they started recording *The Blue Room EP* with Chris Allison, that producer saw startling signs that the band's singer was – behind the oft-quoted boyish bravado and buoyant optimism – crushingly self-critical: "Well, going on my experience with him, Chris was always going to do something amazing because he was such a determined and bright individual. He could have turned his hand to anything and done well at it. He was the major instigator for most stuff that went on in the studio at that time and his presence was pretty powerful over the rest of the group.

"Whether it was his personality or whether it was the stressful situation he was put under, he got quite paranoid about his vocals. Quite unnecessarily, because a lot of the time his vocals were really, *really* good, but he had this constant concern whether they were good enough. He was literally saying 'I am crap, I am useless', to the opposite extreme. There might have been a few little lines to correct here and there, or he could have sung [something] slightly better, but for someone to say 'It all sounds shit, my voice is crap' was just… maybe it was the stress, maybe it's his personality to go to that extent, to make a point. But he was also very keen on doing a complete vocal take… even if you dropped him in for a chorus or a couple of lines on a verse, rather than keep it sounding good like that, he'd want to do the whole vocal take from scratch, taking another track and seeing if he could get it all in one go. Which is commendable, but not entirely necessary."

It wasn't just in the studio that Chris was often very hard on himself. At *NME*'s Brat Awards in February 2001, industry insiders were perplexed by Chris's behaviour and series of seemingly bizarre acceptance speeches. He was visibly nervous and eventually ended up running out of the venue in Shoreditch, east London before the end of the ceremony.

Coldplay had won three awards, but this seemed to settle Chris's nerves not one iota. The first award, for the Radio 1 '*Evening Session Of The Year*', went without a hitch but as he collected their second award, for 'Best New Artist', Chris made a passing reference to British soulster Craig David. In particular he mocked his hairstyle, likening it to a cauliflower. It was hardly one of rock's greatest slurs, but no sooner had the words escaped from his mouth than Chris was mortified at having uttered a slight against a man he didn't even know. While Craig David probably just laughed it off, Chris dwelt on it and became deeply upset with himself. As he collected the 'Best Single' award, he apologised and shortly afterwards made a rapid exit from the venue, running towards Liverpool Street Station where his girlfriend later found him alone.

His explanation for this erratic behaviour served only to highlight his insecurities: "I got there and I was sat among Oasis, Radiohead and U2 and I felt like this little kid, I didn't know what I was doing. Then I had to get the awards and I was terrified... I keep thinking lots of people are out to get us, when they aren't. I get paranoid."

After the second award, when his demeanour had worsened, Chris had convinced himself that he had been "rude about Bono" and in deference to the Irish rocker for whom Chris has the utmost respect, he felt he had put himself in "some sort of nightmare". Yet his speeches contained no such comments and no bystanders overheard anything about Bono either. Even Chris himself was confused, not sure if he had actually said or imagined saying it, or whether it was all down to jet lag. "I wanted to say, 'We're doing well and we've got a new album on the way.' But it came out as this garbled nonsense. I hadn't eaten all day and I had some champagne, when I don't normally drink much. I drank it out of fear." Even the much-regretted Craig David remark was askew, with Chris admitting, "I don't know what that was about. I meant to say Brussels sprouts and it came out as cauliflower. Everything came out wrong."

There were other extenuating circumstances. Chris had fallen in love around the time of *Parachutes* but the relationship had not lasted, leaving him badly hurt. Other reports suggested Chris was concerned that his hair was falling out. He seemed to be in a constant state of self-doubt about whether people liked his band, and confessed to being mortified about how insignificant it all seemed when taken in the context of the world's wider problems.

More worryingly, he said that he often felt that the next day could be his last and that he sometimes went around saying goodbye to people, just in case. Will watched with growing unease: "Chris was going through mad paranoia and everyone was fucking worried."

No one was more worried than Chris Martin. He was worried about the rigours of touring so much; worried about not being able to write better material; worried about what people think about the band, about him, about their songs; worried that they might just have one hit album and then implode; worried about being worried.

Chris was not the only member of Coldplay to experience personal traumas during this period. For Will, matters were much, *much* worse. On the day the band completed *Parachutes*, his mother had died. Yet, because he had a happy childhood and came from a secure family, this did not seem to merit any sympathy. This hit hard, of course. "I can't say I had a harsh childhood, but I've had a lot of things to deal with, especially in the last year. People say, 'You haven't suffered'. It's like, 'Fuck you, you don't know what I've been through.'" (Later, in 2006, Will would open a state-of-the-art new archaeology building at Southampton University, which contained a seminar room named in honour of his late mother.)

Jon and Guy had problems of their own. Jon had contracted glandular fever and was bedridden for much of the promotional work for the album, and totally out of action for a month, missing the Mercury Music Prize ceremony altogether. Guy was also becoming unsettled, talking with Chris about how he thought the album was a shambles. At one stage, Chris hadn't done a print interview for months. He'd always said that talking about their music seemed pointless, unnecessary to him. Creating it was all that mattered.

This was understandable in one sense, but also unrealistic. Chris was now part of a global corporate machine, which would constantly solicit media interest and process endless requests for interviews. This was a necessary evil for all rock stars, especially for those at the beginning of their careers, but it did not sit well with Chris or the band. "This is not what we got into a band to do," said Will. "We're not orators. That's why we play music. There's something inherent in the music that can't be said, something that exists outside of speech."

On top of it all, Chris had become preoccupied with the fact that their commitments had prevented him from writing any new material. By the end of their European tour in the summer of 2001 he hadn't written a new song in months. They were beginning to feel spent, emotionally and creatively.

Ironically, it seemed that as *Parachutes* became more and more successful in all parts of the globe, so Coldplay's difficulties increased. Rumours quickly began circulating that they were not coping well. On the road, Jon was reading *Das Boot*, a novel about the gradual and horrific mental breakdown of a troop of German submariners; the band quickly dubbed their own tour bus Das Bus in sympathy.

Other reports had them announcing they would do no more interviews, "either because we won't have to – because we'll be so massive – or because we'll have been dropped". They regularly cited the "Crispian Mills syndrome" – referring to the lead singer of the ill-fated Kula Shaker, who enjoyed generally strong praise and reasonable commercial success until a throwaway comment about Hitler saw Mills pilloried in the press and his band's career effectively terminated.

Some journalists felt Coldplay's attitude towards the media was simply too defensive. For a band that had suffered virtually no protracted bad press, certainly nothing on the level of personal attacks and scathing criticism that some bands suffer, certain comments did little to endear them to their (few) critics. An example, from Chris: "That's what hurts – when people criticise you and dismiss all your effort in just a couple of thoughtless lines. Every time I read something which attacks us, even if it's only a tiny little thing in an article not about us, it gets me there. It's upsetting, but it makes you more determined."

For many critics, this was simply just a young bunch of former students griping about the troubles of fame. Worse still, they'd only done one album, a few tours, and some press campaigning. What about those rock veterans who'd been in the spotlight for decades, toured the world countless times and endured the white heat of the media in their private and business lives since their careers began? Who was going to empathise with a band whose only problem could be said to be getting too many great reviews?

To his credit, Guy acknowledged how absurd their complaints might seem, telling Q magazine: "I hate bands that moan, but there was no learning curve. It was a vertical gradient. I can remember meeting Sylvester Stallone in LA because he wanted to use 'Trouble' on the soundtrack for his film. We said 'No', but we were a student band being back-slapped by Sylvester Stallone. We thought, 'How the fuck did we get here?'"

Yet, some context is needed here. This is hardly a foursome of eccentrics, outcasts from *One Flew Over The Cuckoo's Nest*. They had only been a band for three years. Now they were being feted by all manner of celebrities. They had their self-doubts, but this was hardly a fault – indeed it is a refreshing change from the norm of bands playing the Bull & Gate in Kentish Town and announcing to the assembled 120 people that "We are the best band in the world!" That said, in typically self-effacing mood, Chris did manage to suggest they *might* be "one of the 10 best bands in the world". Their live and promotional work rate had been fairly extreme since signing to Parlophone. Will had lost his mom. Chris had had his heart broken. And let's not forget that before Coldplay's success they were students, whose sole purpose in life is usually not to work.

A further unwelcome aspect of life for Coldplay was adverse comment relating to their relatively privileged upbringings, which, virtually since their inception, had been thrown at them as if to somehow invalidate their songs and their work. The band themselves were totally bored of the whole question and, to be fair, it was rather tiresome. The concept that poverty was essential to the making of a true artist, that it was necessary to suffer for your art, that a comfortable background was anathema to genuine creativity, was just a cliché, especially in rock and pop. Moreover, this promotes the ludicrous suggestion that, if you are jilted or a love is unrequited, provided you go to a good school or your dad drives a nice car, it doesn't hurt as much. Absurd.

For a start, this school of thought has little basis in fact. The long history of rock and pop offers countless examples of quite brilliant artists whose upbringings were far from destitute. John Lennon might have been raised by an aunt but it was in the comfort of a nice middle-class, semi-detached home. Mick Jagger's dad was a PE teacher and his mum a cosmetics salesperson, so they were hardly dunking stale bread in water. Jim Morrison's dad was a well-to-do career naval officer. Pete Townshend's father was himself a successful professional musician while his mother kept an antique shop. Two of Pink Floyd came from very wealthy families while 'tortured genius' Syd Barrett, the son of a doctor, was decidedly middle-class. Genesis formed at Charterhouse public school. Nick Drake's father was in the Foreign Service while Robert Plant's was an accountant. Bowie's dad was an administrator for Barnado's and Elton John was also middle-class. Even Bob Dylan was the son of a man who ran a successful electrical and furniture store. Moreover, much of the music business and the media that centres around it is populated by decidedly middle-class people.

It wasn't until the emergence of punk in the mid-Seventies that anyone gave much thought to the social backgrounds of rock and pop stars, by which time those who'd tasted success had adopted all the trappings of the middle- and upper-classes anyway. It was this distance between the stars and their fans that enraged the punks more than anything else and inspired them to vilify established bands as 'old farts'. The natural consequence of this class friction was that questions about social backgrounds were now asked as a matter of routine, with deep suspicion falling on those would-be rockers from middle-class homes. Thus "difficult childhoods" and "council estate upbringing" became *de rigueur* for the architects of punk though there were notable exceptions, with reasonably affluent backgrounds doing nothing whatsoever to dilute the impact of Joe Strummer and Hugh Cornwell.

Leapfrogging into the era of Coldplay, artists deemed not to have "suffered enough" often found themselves on the receiving end of caustic remarks that had absolutely nothing to do with their music. New Yorkers The Strokes, whose lead singer Julian Casablancas was the son of the millionaire founder of the Elite model agency, were constantly derided because of their privileged backgrounds. Julian and fellow Stroke Albert Hammond, the son of a successful songwriter, first met in Switzerland at Institut Le Rosey, one of the world's oldest private schools, a haven for children of the world's super-rich.

This type of criticism is nonsense, of course. The Strokes – like Coldplay – write about relationships, about emotional loss, about experiences that are valid for themselves and their fans regardless of their financial circumstances. This is not to suggest that those artists who have experienced a harrowing upbringing cannot draw something positive from it, just that it's not some mandatory requirement.

Nonetheless, Coldplay found that during the campaign to promote their first few singles and début album, they were constantly being asked the same question: are you just rich little college boys playing at rock stardom? "They became whipping boys," Simon Williams of Fierce Panda opines. "That generation does that. I think Keane get a lot worse. A lot of it is pure ignorance. I am sure I probably do the same thing with bands when I don't know the back story and the struggle. Luckily with Coldplay I do know the story – I saw them play all those gigs. I have a lot of admiration and respect for them. There is snobbery. That is a residual effect from the Seventies and Eighties… but I don't think the band have ever been denying that [background]. I much prefer their approach.

"I saw the toilet in their student digs and it was pretty clear they weren't spending £100 a week on a cleaner. They were living the student dream! They were very level-headed young men. They certainly didn't sit there talking about the weekend playing polo. If you sat down with Chris Martin [back then] he'd be asking you questions about the music business. They slummed it in every possible sense too; on tour they played [tiny gigs]. I find Coldplay a far more valid indie band than a lot of bands today, who are so up their own arses [that] you offer them a gig and they are worth 20 people in Shoreditch and the first response is 'How much do we get?' Coldplay were one of the last genuine generational bands."

Of course, in typical Coldplay fashion, Chris Martin saw in this yet another reason to experience self-doubt, as he admitted to *The Observer*. "I'd think: 'Gosh, I'm just some public-school boy with my house colours. I've got a degree. I'm from a middle-class family in Devon. I've got no story. We're just a bunch of students. I don't drink, I don't take drugs, I don't smoke. I can't be compared with Liam Gallagher or The Sex Pistols, or anyone real. I haven't got any experiences as valid as the Wu Tang Clan.' I was incredibly insecure about it."

CHAPTER 10

Spending Time With
Uncle Sam (Inc.)

Since the British invasion of the USA that followed the arrival of The Beatles in 1964, every British band with talent and ambition has seen America as some sort of Monte Cristo, Alexander Dumas' mythical island where Edmond Dantes discovered the vast horde of hidden treasure that transformed his life. It takes brutal hard work to crack America, as well as talent, and those who do manage it can invariably be found occupying large country houses, not necessarily in the land of their birth. The late Sixties and early Seventies was the golden era for British bands in America but the post-punk pickings have been harder to snatch.

Though not British, U2 managed it, as did Depeche Mode. Oasis didn't, at least not on the same scale, while Travis, Stereophonics and Blur sank without trace. The Prodigy's fire-starting dance-punk did it with the 10-million-selling *The Fat Of The Land*. Week after week sees the ever-optimistic *NME* hail a new band, British or otherwise, as having "cracked" the States or "taken America by storm". One such report had The Vines down as "invading" the USA because their album had gone in the *Billboard* charts at number 77. Meanwhile, N Sync and Eminem can shift more than two million albums in *one week*. That's cracking America.

Thus it was that Coldplay turned their attentions to America. It might have seemed wishful thinking on their part to hope to make an impact in the US only months after releasing *Parachutes*, but its success had been so *total* in the UK that there were certainly grounds for cautious optimism. Indeed, small quantities of the album had already been imported into the US and were being snapped up eagerly. The process began by signing to Nettwerk Records, a subsidiary of EMI that was allied to an influential management company, home also to Avril Lavigne.

One of Coldplay's first US engagements was at Los Angeles radio station KROQ's annual Christmas show, where they played on a revolving stage in front of about 8,000 fans. Suitably inspired, they spent the rest of the week in LA, including dinner engagements with Moby and Thora Birch. The real tour to promote the album was due to commence in the spring of 2001, with this trip a brief taster of the work that was to come.

The first US single was 'Yellow', which came out Stateside in November and soon attracted heavy radio play. US record buyers rarely embrace a band that has not conquered American radio, so this was a good start. In 2002 the most popular genre of radio in America was country & western, but the normally conservative stations took to the Coldplay sound straight away. They had got off to a flyer.

The album was released just after 'Yellow', while the band was still busy promoting the record in the UK and Europe. The US media was impressed, though they were not quite as fawning as the UK press had been. Nonetheless, MTV declared that Coldplay's "sublime pleasures tend to creep up on listeners. Martin's cheeriness lends levity to the British quartet's set [with its] ethereal sound." Amazon.com called it "a wonderfully assured début". Unfortunately, it was not until February in the new year that they were finally able to start touring America and capitalise on this momentum.

Once again, 'Yellow' had proved pivotal and they knew it: "We've done practically nothing in terms of playing live there," said Guy. "The radio stations just went mad for it ['Yellow']. We're lucky to miss that initial treadmill of playing the toilet circuit." To their immense credit, Travis had already toured heavily around the USA to promote their *The Man Who* album and actually took copies of 'Yellow' to radio stations, telling them of the song's success in the UK. Although the Scottish band enjoyed some popularity, particularly on the student circuit, they certainly did not crack America. When Coldplay later arrived in the US to begin their own campaign, they found countless doors already open due to Travis' generous support.

Coldplay thus leapfrogged the lesser circuits and found themselves playing venues such as The Fillmore in San Francisco and Irving Plaza in New York. In turn, this gave the impression that they were much bigger Stateside than their modest sales suggested. One benefit was that their hotels on the road varied from modest to luxurious, as against the $20-a-night hovels that so many Brit bands have to endure on their early US tours. Chris still took exception to American TV, in particular the adverts, and found the whole culture fascinating yet revolting.

They played a dozen North American dates in the spring of 2001 and then returned in late May for another 16 shows, then seven more in December of that year, and sales of *Parachutes* in the US were boosted by yet another strong radio single, 'Shiver'. This was a solid start albeit far removed from the three years of solid touring that they had been led to believe would be required.

In mid-August, 2002, just prior to the release of their second album, Coldplay played arguably their most high-profile US gig to date, at New York's famous Bowery Ballroom. They again faced a crowd of thousands, among who were the Gallagher brothers (and Hollywood superstar actress Gwyneth Paltrow). The first mention of Oasis came with a reference to Noel's recent car crash, Chris dedicating 'God Put A Smile On Your Face' to "anybody who's been in a car accident recently".

With the set apparently finished, Chris suggested that anyone who wanted a few surprises might stay behind. He then returned and sat down at the piano to sing 'Songbird', written by Liam Gallagher for his wife, Nicole Appleton, formerly of All Saints (at the time a member of the duo Appleton with her sister Natalie). This tribute brought the relationship with Oasis full circle from that night way back when Liam told Chris that 'Yellow' had made him want to write songs again. Onlookers reported that Noel Gallagher jumped to his feet and cheered loudly when Chris struck up the opening chords of his brother's song. Chris then closed the show with another cover, this time Echo & The Bunnymen's 'Lips Like Sugar'.

A few days later, in Los Angeles, the star-studded crowds included both Jack Nicholson and Minnie Driver. Chris dedicated 'Everything's Not Lost' to "all the actors and actresses in the house" and even changed the lyrics to: "And if you haven't won an Oscar, and you think that all is lost." Other celebrity fans spotted at Coldplay gigs have included Sean Penn, Heather Graham, Puff Daddy, Justin Timberlake, Brad Pitt and Elton John.

With UK sales heading towards the two million mark, *Parachutes'* US progress would almost double that within a few months. By the end of 2001, they had shifted 500,000, but by the summer of 2002 that had rocketed to 1.75 million copies in the US alone. Soon after, they won a prestigious Grammy for 'Best Alternative Album'. All this, coupled with UK sales and the modest but positive quantities sold in other countries such as Japan and parts of Europe, meant that by the time the band were ready to release their follow-up record, the début album had managed a staggering 5.5 million copies. Remember that original target of 40,000? EMI must have been mildly pleased.

As America came increasingly under Coldplay's spell, their infamous insistence on controlling every aspect of everything to do with the band became more and more difficult to maintain. This fierce control manifests itself in many different ways. Coldplay took the photograph for the cover of their début album themselves; after their early studio difficulties they agreed to co-produce every record; they are central to the design and artwork of every sleeve of every release; they take control of every video, from concept to direction; they rarely allow any Coldplay track to be used on advertisements or film soundtracks despite several extremely lucrative offers, with a few notable charity-based exceptions. Interestingly, in March of 2003, the track 'Clocks' was being used on ITV to advertise a new drama called *William And Mary*. There were also snippets of Coldplay tracks used on the comedy drama *Cold Feet* and even on news bulletins. In 2003, Chris said, "Now we've asked that we are not even informed of the [corporate advertising] offers any more. We just turn them down straight away. I know we could divert the money offered into worthwhile causes, but we'd be cheating the people who bought our records, wouldn't we?" It is said they have turned down offers in excess of £4 million from American soft-drink manufacturers

Gatorade (for 'Yellow') and Diet Coke (for 'Trouble') for example. This will have been repeated many times over.

Whether Coldplay can maintain this control remains to be seen. Younger bands often make similarly strident statements, but soften later in their careers when capitalising on their assets seems like a comfortable option. The same applies to sponsorship of tours, which at one stage was seen as the epitome of the sell-out culture but is almost commonplace on the modern gig circuit. Certainly, it has backfired for some artists – when Moby allowed every track of his multi-platinum selling album *Play* to be used as advertising and/or soundtracks, there was a fiery backlash accusing him of blatant commercialisation.

Yet, exercised with caution and in moderation, it is doubtful if licensing of material for outside use has any real effect on a band's status, other than financial. Film soundtracks are a similar case in point. Many major bands from U2 to Prodigy to Limp Bizkit and countless others have allowed their music to be used in movies without any negative impact on their credibility whatsoever. Since the days of Trent Reznor's remarkable soundtrack to Oliver Stone's controversial *Natural Born Killers*, the role of the soundtrack – and the bands that play a part in that – has been turned on its head.

While it's unlikely that Coldplay would 'do a Brian May' and write lyrics for Ford adverts ("Look at this car, look how it shines for you, and everything you do, and it is all Ford"), selective approval in cases where quality control is exercised seems to harm no one.

Nonetheless, at this stage in their careers, Coldplay remained adamant: "It's been all on our own terms," states Will. "We have 100 per cent control over any aspect of whatever we do, and that's really important to who we are and the music we make… We're not a band that can be pushed around, although we do have some amazing advisors."

Whatever their thoughts about exploiting their music for financial gain, Coldplay are happy to use it to promote fair trade with impoverished Third World countries and assist work with other charities such as The Future Forest and Amnesty International. Tellingly, they refused to supply music to a coffee company that they believed exploited cheap Third World labour.

While Coldplay had yet go to the lengths of more high-profile rock campaigners like Bob Geldof or Bono, they have always felt an obligation to raise the profile of particular issues, to make people aware. "Our job isn't really to offer solutions," explains Chris, "as much as it is to advertise the whole issue. We're not trying to get on a pedestal, we're just using whatever media we can to interest people."

The most involved early example of the band's commitment to Make Trade Fair was Chris Martin's visit to Haiti and the Dominican Republic in 2002. The tour of farming communities was sponsored and backed by Oxfam with the goal of persuading richer nations to alter their debilitating trade laws (Chris was initially put in touch with Oxfam by Emily Eavis, whose dairy farmer father, Michael, runs the Glastonbury Festival). This was no five-star celebrity tour bus, no rider, no fawning fans and no press adulation. It was day after day of dirt tracks, malaria-infested jungle and exposure to destitute rural communities; not destitute as in struggling to make their social benefits last until next week – destitute as in "about to die". The trek took Chris to many villages whose residents have been severely economically (and by consequence in every aspect of their lives) deprived by unfair international trade laws. This means that the highly volatile coffee market, for example, which can fluctuate from one hour to the next in the hi-tech world of the 21st century stock market, can flip these people's lives on their heads without them even knowing.

The gruelling but insightful trip made a deep and disturbing impact. "It was like all the stuff I learned about in geography lessons wasn't just bullshit," he said. "It was real, all the deforestation and exploitation. It's going on and it's fucking horrific. When you see people whose lives are affected and you are responsible, it's like being kicked in the head." He also told a reporter from *The Sun*, "It was amazing, unlike anything I've ever done before. We spent days in the back of a pick-up truck, covered in dust. It made me feel grateful and even more driven for us not to waste our opportunity. It was a big kick up the arse. I met this guy who couldn't afford a guitar. He could be the next big thing and he hasn't had any opportunity to do anything with his talent. I'm never going to take anything for granted again." In photographs, on TV and at live shows, Chris has since scribbled the words "Make Trade Fair" or that organisation's website address and the two lines of the charity's logo on the back of his hand. He is also in the habit of taping his fingers, a deliberate ploy to draw visual attention to this important logo nearby.

This is not a *cause célèbre* for just Chris – the entire band is behind it. "Anyone in our position has a certain responsibility," explained Guy. "Odd though it may seem to us, a lot of people read what we're saying, see us on TV, buy our records and read the sleeves, and that can be a great platform. You can make people aware of issues. It isn't very much effort for us at all, but if it can help people, then we want to do it."

Very early on in their careers, the band realised the rather ludicrous nature of what they do for a living: "Of course it's rock star conscience," admitted Chris to Q magazine. "I mean, I am loaded! And I love my life! And I'm selfish. I flick through *OK!* magazine and look at the pretty girls and I worry about my reviews and, yes, it's a cosy, cocooned existence. But I've woken up to the shit underneath. When you realise that there are rules keeping people in poverty because they're not allowed to trade, you wake up."

It was a natural progression from advertising the issues in their artwork and interviews to actually performing in support of the cause. Thus Coldplay readily agreed to perform in Trafalgar Square in central London for a charity concert supporting Make Trade Fair. This brought the band full circle really, because this was the scene of where, as a completely unknown band, they had signed their record deal to Parlophone just four years earlier.

Another notable charity the band vehemently support is Water Aid. This cause aims to provide safe and sanitised water in some of the world's poorest countries. The band even invited Water Aid to have stalls at their shows. Oddly, the connection with Coldplay was made when a librarian at South West Water by the name of Chris Martin spoke to Coldplay's singer about the charity. The band have championed the cause ever since.

CHAPTER 11

The Yellow Man

"People want their rock stars to pull up in a limousine. It is what they expect."

Freddy Mercury

"Will is the nicest bloke in the world, but if you take his seat on the bus, then you've had it. This is as aggressive as we get."

Chris Martin

So Coldplay had shifted over five million copies of their début album. They had started to infiltrate America. They were being talked of as *the* next great British rock band. But that wasn't enough. Not only were they apparently a bunch of lightweight school chums with no *real* life experience, said their critics, but perhaps most disturbingly of all, they didn't *rock and roll*.

They didn't appear to take drugs. Groupies seemed rather thin on the ground. Chris openly admitted to barely drinking at all. He didn't smoke either. Not one of them had had the decency to punch a fan or even cancel a gig due to "nervous exhaustion". Worse still, they got on with their parents, were glad they had been educated well and – most depressingly of all – they were generally "nice". They were certainly not the saviours of debauched rock 'n' roll. What did this mean for the future of British music?

Oasis had reintroduced the outrage into rock 'n' roll. While the likes of Travis and Radiohead appeared utterly incapable of, or rather disinterested in, overstepping the mark, the Gallagher brothers made it an art form. Countless fights among themselves, with photographers, bodyguards, swearing, profane gestures, inflammatory remarks, boozing, drug use, leggy blondes – they went for the full Monty.

Not so Coldplay. Their rougher edges were more like softly sanded curves. They wore casual clothes, trainers, no outrageous haircuts, no tattoos saying "I hate me" or genital piercings (as far as we know). They did start to think too much about their image in the aftermath of *Parachutes* but quickly realised the futility and transparency of that. They cited bands such as Kraftwerk, who were virtually unknowns on the street, as musical pioneers.

Their conservatism was not restricted to their appearance. Of course, this is not a quartet of Cliff Richards. Guy and Will smoke Marlboro (Lights). They all drink, albeit Chris sparsely. However, excessive nights out are few and far between. Chris didn't drink much simply because he didn't like being out of control or the taste of alcohol.

Select magazine summed Coldplay up as "so non-toxic as to make Travis seem like darklords of hazchem vitriol". True, this was no *Hammer Of The Gods*, more an alcohol-free picnic in the park. This was one band who, if they did too much 'coke' would just get wind from the fizzy cola, where the only mainline they were involved in was the one that ran from London to the studio in Liverpool and for whom the word excess often meant they had packed too many literary classics in their suitcases.

While Julio Iglesias boasts of bedding over 3,000 women and any rock band worth their salt dreams of dressing rooms crammed with scantily clad women, Chris offered this little gem about his own fantasies: "I'd like to take [Hollywood actress] Rachel Weisz to fly a kite on Hampstead Heath. That would be cosy."

Chris even admitted that in his college days he often liked nothing more than to go to the library and bury his head in the Bible. He once apologised to his father in the audience for taking the Lord's name "in vain" after a fan pointed out that Mr Christian is an anagram of his name. Chris's faith, albeit apparently diluted somewhat in recent times, was inherited from his devout mother, and he was clearly uncomfortable with the dichotomy of morals his career in such a fiery profession created. On the one hand, he was a young man in the band of the moment, so girls were always around. On the other, he remains convinced that casual sex always causes hurt for someone.

He didn't stop there, admitting to playing Scrabble on the tour bus with his girlfriend and killing spare time by jamming country & western songs. 'Yellow' he likened not to an orgasm or a drug high, but to "a nice cake". When interviewed by one magazine and desperate to get out and about, Chris suggested (over two vanilla milkshakes) a visit to his 15-year-old brother's school sports day or, better still – and hold on to your hats – more kite-flying: "I've got two good ones. It's terrific fun."

Sometimes the band didn't care about what people thought. "I like nothing more after a hard day's work," scoffed a sarcastic Chris during one interview, "than to do loads of coke, meet some local whores and slag off Alan McGee for half an hour. Before listening to Slipknot and swearing about how good Radiohead are, and how we should be more like them ..." They even christened their approach "reverse rock 'n' roll", saying that if the definition of rock 'n' roll was "the seeking of the ultimate pleasure", then hanging out together and writing music was their nirvana.

At heart, and to their distinction, Coldplay never once pretended to be something they were not. Yet the odd thing is, what else did people expect? Three of them were graduates, the sort of people who make your heart sink when you see them at the local pub quiz, halves of shandy at the ready, all buoyant and knowing like a caricature of a team of *University Challenge* contestants. Here was a band that made their name playing introspective ballads and sophisticated, emotionally charged, melodic rock. "We are being rock stars," Chris continued. "We do it *our* way. I'm not going to take off my top and wear leather trousers. It's been done. We're not your classic rock stars by any means. We're not into mainlining crack or smoking our own blood."

Chris told *X Ray* magazine that, "I will lamp any idiot who says we're not rock 'n' roll, because they're fucking idiots. I keep seeing, 'Oh, he's so boring, he just flies kites'. That's what I want to do! I fly kites and I go running! It's geeky but it's also what I want to do."

They do it for the music, man, which does sound incredibly earnest but at the same time is refreshingly honest. The extent to which they provide rock 'n' roll's polar opposite is epitomised by the fact that when Chris was once asked what they had done that people might be interested in, he answered, "Will's a good swimmer." There's something stunningly honest and, by definition, immensely appealing about that answer.

The world tour for *Parachutes* seemed to go on forever. Fatigue was inevitably setting in. At one later point, Chris revealed that he couldn't really listen to *Parachutes* any longer and might only put it on occasionally to impress someone! The rigours of the road were much more serious though. During the American dates in the spring of 2001, perhaps inevitably, Chris lost his voice. The highly anticipated New York gig (February 16, 2001) had to be cut short because of this and during a performance on *Late Nite With Conan O' Brian*, Chris was visibly uncomfortable (the cancelled US shows were rescheduled for late May 2001). They also pulled the plug on dates in Boston, Toronto and Miami. Later, a notice was placed on the official website saying Chris was suffering from "voice exhaustion". Unfortunately, the American dates were not the only ones to be hit. All of Coldplay's forthcoming European tour dates throughout April were cancelled. A specialist throat doctor who examined Chris warned that any more gigs at present could "result in total voice loss and could cause permanent damage". Matters were made worse by Guy catching a particularly bad bout of flu.

This was not the first time this had happened – a show in Edinburgh the previous autumn was cancelled for the same reason. Some claimed it was overwork, others that it was stress-related. This prompted Chris to taking technical singing lessons in order to strengthen his vocal chords (he started off by agreeing with the vocal teacher that he was "shit"). When the rescheduled dates were played, Chris repeatedly sprayed his throat with medicine, chuckling to himself on one occasion before telling the audience, "I should say this is cocaine, just to spice things up a bit."

It appeared, however, that behind the medical annoyances, Chris was experiencing another bout of lost confidence. He was mixing with mega-stars and selling millions of albums, yet still his personal demons caused him to question his worthiness. He was clearly worried about being labelled as "that 'Yellow' man".

In an interview with *Melody Maker* Chris's uncertainty was clear: "No, in a nutshell, it's not easy to deal with ... It's just kind of scary, really. What's changed the most? Our state of mind. It's a very confusing time. I haven't been happy for ages." Fortunately, Jon sat him down and told him to stop the self-doubt, stop the apologies – often from the actual stage each night – and start enjoying himself. His comments hit the mark. "That's the riddle," says Chris. "I think I'm crap, which drives me. But I also think we're brilliant. Once we'd decided we had the chance of a lifetime, we worked harder than we ever have in our lives."

Although they were at times exhausted on the road, playing live was the *modus operandi* for Coldplay. Talking to *Flavour.Lookon.Net*, Chris said: "I hate all the rubbish food we eat when we're touring! But we absolutely love playing together, it's all we really care about. When the four of us play something together, something that we've made that nobody else can do, then I don't care how many hours I have to sit on a shitty tour bus or how many rubbish pasties I have to eat because when we get there and do the show it's great. It's why we're here, and I wouldn't change it for anything."

May 2001 saw the band kick off yet another sell-out UK tour. This was notable mostly for the fact that Chris played an electric guitar on stage for the first time in years. As if to announce the move to a more aggressive instrument, he even threw his acoustic guitar into the crowd, causing an understandable scrum between genuine memento-seeking fans and people with their eyes on the prize of an eBay goldmine. Whereas before they had ended their shows with the Bond theme tune, later in 2001 they started concluding the set with Chris playing a solo cover of Hal David and Burt Bacharach's classic 'What The World Needs Now Is Love' on the piano. Their own headline dates were supplemented by another appearance at the V Festival alongside such acts as a newly recharged Red Hot Chili Peppers and the rather more unchallenging

Texas. Their buoyant mood was boosted by the news they had been nominated for the prestigious 46th annual Ivor Novello Awards for the cumbersomely titled 'The Best Song Musically And Lyrically Award' for 'Trouble', pitching them against S Club 7's 'Never Had A Dream Come True' and David Gray's 'Babylon'.

Fortunately, the band again managed to pull themselves back from the brink. It was probably a mixture of elements that helped them turn the corner. They became acclimatised to the media attention, while physically and mentally they grew accustomed to the rigours of the road. They realised that as long as they delivered what they considered to be quality music, there would be detractors who would struggle to pick away at their admittedly soft underbelly. And they started to become ever more involved in issues beyond the often self-indulgent world of music, like the Make Trade Fair campaign. In difficult times, this could always deliver a short, sharp shock of reality.

Besides, they had their secret weapon up their sleeve. A song. One that was actually written at the very end of the sessions for *Parachutes* but had missed the deadline by a matter of days. They knew it was a classic, they knew this was the very hook that could pluck them out of their hole. That song was called 'In My Place'.

CHAPTER 12

Mac The Knife

Question: *"Any tracks we should be looking out for?"*
Chris Martin: *"Nope. It's all rubbish."*

C hris Martin belongs to the school of thought that believes songs are "given" to writers, that they are somehow floating around and the writer doesn't compose them so much as pluck them from the ether. He is thus not so much a composer as the channel through which the song finds its way to its audience. It's a concept shared with both Paul Simon, and Keith Richards of The Rolling Stones, a belief that has its roots in historical philosophy, where competing academics have for years debated on the role of humans in the world, arguing for and against fatalism as opposed to self-determination. In this sense, and in its most extreme form, Chris's views go completely against everything else he says about his band, suggesting that he and the three other members of Coldplay are in fact no more than lucky bystanders in someone else's grander scheme.

Yet what about the work involved in getting a song out there? What about the production, the choice of instrumentation and so on? Clearly this cannot apply to the entire workings of the complicated machine that is a global rock band?

"When 'Yellow' arrived, I thought, 'Bloody hell. I can't believe we've got that song. That'll be a single.'" Chris claims that most of the words and all of the melody came to him at the same time, and that he had been "blessed" by this arrival.

Yet he also acknowledged, during an internet Q&A, that the band's personal decisions can hugely affect the final sound of a song. "Then it becomes exciting because then it starts to become Coldplay. Jonny starts putting riffs on it to make it better. That's what being in a band is all about. I'll come in with the start of a song and it's what everyone else puts on it that makes it a Coldplay song." Just as well, otherwise you could argue that all Coldplay did was place themselves in the right place at the right time to catch these classic songs.

This goes some way to explain their decision to pull back from the brink of soft-metal hell. Before their career had really taken off, they had experimented with some rockier, more metal sounds but thankfully they saw the error of their ways and diverted off into far more sophisticated territory. Having said that, Chris claims the only reason these fledgling efforts were never committed to tape was because "luckily, we weren't allowed in the studio then. Otherwise, we would have made a very bad version of *Back In Black*."

He continued, "It's a good day when you stop worrying about what people think you don't sound like and just worry about what you think you should sound like ... there was a phase when we were thinking, 'Right, we'll show them'. We were butchering all these songs, but then eventually we decided we should do the songs in the way that they should be done and not just plug everything into 12."

The subject matter of Coldplay songs is deeply intertwined with Chris's frame of mind. He has admitted he needs to be slightly morose, maudlin even, to write well. He cannot see how he can write if he is in a serious and happily committed relationship. Much of this he credits to his father, who he says is a terrible worrier.

Chris credits Will's willingness to put forward critical opinions as one of Coldplay's major strengths. Reciprocally, it is Chris's readiness to accept this criticism that allows their song ideas to develop as they do. Such candidness can lead to strife but as a general rule the band claim that sarcasm and insults are their favourite method of objecting to a particular track, lyric or sound.

★

Before finally starting work on the follow-up album to *Parachutes*, Coldplay had one enormo-gig in particular to play: supporting U2 at the 80,000 capacity Slane Castle on August 25. Chris had even invited the beautiful former child-model-turned-*Neighbours*-star-turned-pop-star-turned-cosmetics-model Natalie Imbruglia to the show. Even more thrilling than this was the amazing moment when, halfway through U2's set, Bono segued a few bars of 'Yellow' into his own band's 'Bad'.

Coldplay started work on their second album in October 2001, following a hectic 12-month period promoting *Parachutes* that had seen them playing gigs every month since the previous October, many of them in the USA and Australasia. After the Slane Castle date, the band enjoyed a rare few weeks off before heading into the studio to start recording a follow-up to an album that had by now sold over five million copies. Chris openly admitted he hadn't written any new songs for months. At first, this scarcity of new ideas crippled the band. Chris even thought Coldplay might be finished.

But all was not lost. At the very end of the last sessions, Chris was tinkering around on an old pump organ that a friend had leant to him. He was mimicking Jimmy Cliff and Procol Harum's 'Whiter Shade Of Pale' but the antiquated pedals and peculiar sound of the organ reminded him of drunken sailors, so he amused himself by trying to play a mock-sea shanty. The chords became the backbone of a new song, quickly christened 'In My Place'. It seemed magical, but since *Parachutes* had already been delivered to the mastering room this new song was filed away for future reference.

Two years later, desperate for new material, Coldplay dusted off and re-recorded this hangover track from the first album to see if it could get the ball rolling. What they captured on tape was, in their opinion, "the best thing we've ever written". Suddenly Coldplay were back on track. A wave of optimism and creative momentum flooded over them. Within days they had a long list of songs in progress, including working titles such as 'A Ghost', 'Your Guess Is As Good As Mine', 'Deserter', 'Fingers Crossed', 'Amsterdam', 'Murder', 'This Hollow Frame', 'In My Place', 'Animals' and 'In Isolation'.

The production team was the same as for the previous album, with

Ken Nelson co-producing with the band, alongside the computer programming skills of Mark Phythain. Progress was steady with the band attending the sessions with almost military discipline. Indeed, they felt like they were at a nine-to-five job at times, but nonetheless the progress was swift and smooth.

By Christmas the recordings were finished. The problem was, everyone was happy – except the band. With record company executives visibly breaking out into a sweat, the band decided not to release those sessions as they were and instead headed back to Liverpool's Parr Street studio, where much of *Parachutes* had been completed, to effectively start again. Eschewing the multi-personnel of a big London studio, just the élite six of the band, Ken and Mark entrenched themselves behind the desk and locked the door behind them. This intense gang-like mentality started working immediately.

Consequently, some songs, with titles such as 'Animals' (which had proved popular when previewed on tour), 'Idiot', 'I Ran Away' and 'Murder', were actually trashed altogether. "There was a feeling it was almost going too smoothly," explained Jon. "We were pleased with it, but then we took a step back and realised that it wasn't right. It would have been easy to say we'd done enough, to release an album to keep up the momentum, but we didn't. And I'm glad because now we have something we'll be happy to tour with for two years." A whole two years? What's this? Coldplay getting complacent?

Within two weeks, a batch of great new songs had been recorded, including 'Daylight', 'A Whisper' and 'The Scientist'. "We just felt completely inspired, and felt we could do anything we liked. We didn't have to do the acoustic thing, we didn't have to do a loud rock thing, we didn't have to react against anything."

While they were recording the new album, one very famous face was allowed into the inner confines of the otherwise sacrosanct studio – Ian McCulloch of Echo & The Bunnymen. Renowned for his outrageous self-belief and enormous presence, McCulloch remains to this day one of the most charismatic rock stars the UK has ever produced. At the height of the Bunnymen's fame, he was a genuine icon for the new age, and he is still regarded with great reverence and affection by many.

A Liverpudlian through and through, he first met the band in a bar next door to the Parr Street Studios. McCulloch shared a manger with Coldplay's producer Ken Nelson and after a few polite exchanges when Chris nervously tried to buy him a bowl of soup, they eventually shared a drink and struck up an unlikely friendship. Within a few days, McCulloch was enrolled as a sort of unofficial consultant for the album. (Another odd Coldplay fact for these sessions is that one of the dinner ladies at Parr Street studios was in fact Sandi Thom, the singer-songwriter who later had a global smash hit in 2006 with 'I Wish I Was A Punk Rocker'.)

Coldplay invited McCulloch into the studio and welcomed his suggestions about their developing material. It is there for all to see in some of the sounds on the record but it was perhaps Ian's non-musical influence that had the biggest effect on the young band. He was so seasoned, he had seen it all, been to the very top (albeit not in America) and (to a lesser extent) slipped down a little, and they drew great strength from his late-night tales and seemingly bottomless pit of rock 'n' roll pearls of wisdom.

Chris Martin was in his first year of primary school when Echo & The Bunnymen burst on to the world of UK rock with their epic swathes of pop and piercingly effective ballads. Twenty years later, Coldplay extracted from McCulloch the rare admission that they were the band "he would most like to be in today". "He's got it," said McCulloch of Chris. "I want to hate them but they're so good. He's too much of a perfectionist. He should relax. I never enjoyed that level of success and I think they should just try and enjoy it."

Their famous mentor did not just provide ideas and opinions on the material being recorded. For 'In My Place', Chris invited him into the singing booth to sit right next to him and even wore Macca's trademark heavy raincoat. Macca, who had been drinking red wine heavily, just sat listening and occasionally saying, "Go on, son. Go on."

Ian McCulloch oozed self-confidence, the one asset that Chris Martin so often lacked. Spending time with the Liverpudlian legend helped the Coldplay singer feel more assured about what he does, as he told *NME*.com: "I've met various people who've made me more and more

Coldplay: Nobody Said It Was Easy

at peace with what I do musically with my friends. Tim Wheeler, Danny McNamara and other people, but with Mac because he's so infamous and he's so as you expect when you meet him, all cigarettes and sunglasses, you're shit-scared for a bit, but then you realise that what's driving him is the same as what's driving you and your band." Observers commented that Chris somehow had a new swagger in his step that was not there before he met McCulloch.

Macca wasn't the only influence that came to bear on these sessions. The band had been listening to a much more varied array of music since *Parachutes* had taken them on that whirlwind tour of the world. German rockers Rammstein (whom the band also befriended), PJ Harvey, Tom Waits, the hardcore At The Drive-In and the rather more obscure The Blind Boys of Alabama, plus older albums by The Cure and The Rolling Stones were all regulars on the Coldplay CD.

Of course, in typical Coldplay fashion, there were other key factors in keeping their muse primed and inspired for the new songs. Album opener 'Politik' was written on September 13, 2001, just two days after a pair of hijacked passenger jets slammed into the World Trade Center twin towers in New York, in what was a very tangible realisation of modern Armageddon. Also, Chris's own personal relationships were still paramount in his thoughts when writing. On a rather more comical note, his insecurities about his appearance kept bubbling up to the surface too, in particular his fear of going bald.

Over the course of eight months, the album finally began to take shape. There were lengthy and heated debates about almost every aspect of every track, with the drum and bass patterns a special bone of contention. Their obsessive perfectionism often stifled progress, with rumours suggesting they actually used *1,000 hours* of studio time for the 11 songs of the final cut. Yet more touring and Chris's Oxfam excursion also meant this was to remain a lengthy and drawn-out recording process.

Chris was not about to let his anxious record company associates relax. With great excitement about the new album quickly leading to business talk of multi-platinum sales four or five albums down the road, Chris was more than happy to put a spanner in the works, admitting, "We're empty again now. Drained of ideas. Who knows if we'll do it again?" Jon seemed even more doubtful of their longevity: "I honestly can't tell you where another [album] would come from."

Leaks occur in the rock world as much as they do in Whitehall, and these self-doubts somehow escaped into the outside world, leading to rumours on the internet that the band were going to call it a day after the release of the new album. Much of the conjecture centred around quotes attributed to Chris on *NME*.com. Asked about the band's future he said: "As far as I'm concerned this will be the last one we ever make. But I hope that one day we have some more songs, you know? If someone said, 'You've got to start a new album tomorrow,' I'd say, 'I don't think we can do better than this. We'll only do another album if we think it'll be better. I don't really care about the whole 15 album thing. I like the whole Joy Division approach." He even suggested he might become a busker in London's Piccadilly Circus (presumably with ambitions to be more successful than when he and Jonny spectacularly failed the first time they went busking there, pre-Coldplay).

The gossip escalated when the original June 2002 release of the record, scheduled to coincide with a forthcoming Glastonbury headline slot, was delayed because the band wanted to spend more time mixing the finished tapes. Others suggested the band's decision to pre-release the track listing was another sign of uncertainty in the camp – in the Napster-era, actual track names enabled fans to scour the internet trying to download tracks before an official release. So many high-profile acts had fallen foul of this, most recently Oasis, who discovered to their dismay that all 11 tracks from their *Heathen Chemistry* album were already freely available to download over three months prior to the album release.

Such rumours were further fuelled by suggestions that Chris Martin wanted to quit while he was ahead and end the band on a high. His own familiar mumblings in the press about how he could die any minute because of the amount of flying the band were undertaking and how he always viewed every gig and song as their last, added to the confusion.

This was all nonsense of course. Notwithstanding the fact the band had a five-album deal to honour, the rumours really were no more than that, web gossip. The band tried to dampen the speculation by explaining that without very careful mixing of the tracks the whole album could be ruined, a process that was necessarily taking them several weeks. This mixing was finally completed in New York and also in George Martin's Air Studios in London, before the album was finally pencilled in for an autumn 2002 release.

As if to confirm their current status as the UK's biggest rock act, Coldplay headlined their favourite festival, Glastonbury, on Friday, June 28. During this period they also showcased samples from their forthcoming album at the Meltdown Festival at the London Royal Festival Hall in July, hosted this year by David Bowie, who selected the acts to perform. Will even hinted that Bowie might appear on stage with them at one point. He talked of "a surprise guest appearance". Bowie didn't show, but someone else did.

The gig itself was outstanding in such an intimate venue but was perhaps most notable for the interloper who ran on stage during 'Yellow' and took over the vocals. At first the man's identity remained a mystery, which *NME* tried to solve by launching a tongue-in-cheek manhunt for the shy new star. "Who was he? A budding star or a pissed-up twat?"

He was, in fact, Patrick Harvey, a 26-year-old from Birmingham who'd been drinking heavily all afternoon prior to the stage charge. When the band struck up the opening chords of 'Yellow', he joined the hundreds of fans who ran to the front of the stage. As he related to *NME*, "I thought 'I'll have a bit of that', but I went down the right side so I was on my own. I was feeling a bit left out so I thought 'Bollocks to it, I'm getting up on stage, man!' I just bent my leg and up I was! I think someone came on stage to get me and Chris waved him away."

Heartened by the Coldplay frontman's apparent welcome, Harvey plucked the microphone from Chris's hand and sang the remainder of 'Yellow' to fantastic applause. To make the day even better, he was congratulated by Natalie Imbruglia who was in the crowd. "I only did it for a bit of a giggle and never expected it to go as far as it did," he admitted later. Coldplay were unusually relaxed about the entire episode, especially considering that in former times this might have sent Chris into weeks of paranoia. Instead, they commented in the press that "Coldplay were not able to comment as to whether they would be offering Patrick a permanent position in the band."

The 100,000 sell-out Glastonbury headlining slot on the Pyramid Stage in June 2002 was unquestionably the highlight of Coldplay's life thus far, the perfect career-defining moment. Their work with Oxfam earlier in the year had made them even more motivated to play the famous festival again. "We've got to be good because now we've got more responsibility than just our own careers," said Chris. Thoughts of this prestigious gig had actually energised them while writing the new album, and the night itself offered a perfect opportunity to showcase some new material. Their 15-song set, which included a three-song encore, courageously included six tracks off the forthcoming album. Strangely, the audience roared its appreciation at the opening notes of future second album-opener, 'Politik', even though, apart from the band and their close associates, no one else at that point had ever heard it before.

Chris was clearly overwhelmed by the event and told the crowd the band had been preparing for this gig for 25 years. To the great relief of many around Coldplay, Chris was in great spirits, even apologising for not being Rod Stewart – the veteran rocker was due to play the festival later in the weekend. Indeed, Chris's nervous chatter appeared to endear the band to the crowd much more than the seasoned stage rapport of more established acts.

As it had been for Glastonbury headliners Radiohead, Pulp and even Robbie Williams before them, this show was the single moment when all of Coldplay's songs made sense, when tens of thousands of fans sang along to entire songs and when Chris, Will, Guy and Jon seemed almost lost for words amid the euphoria of the crowd. Most remarkably of all, the song that seemed to get the best reception of the night was the penultimate tune and future lead single off the forthcoming album, 'In My Place'. Chris later described the gig as "the most important day of our lives".

Just in case he might start believing his own myth, however, there was a shock waiting for him at the family residence: "After we had headlined Glastonbury and been pampered and told by everyone that we were great, I went back to my parents' house and got in trouble for not putting the milk away." Later, when his dad picked up a copy of *Q* magazine with his son's face beaming out from the front cover, he said, "You must be pleased you got your teeth done, boy."

CHAPTER 13

The Rush Begins

On first listen, Coldplay's second album, *A Rush Of Blood To The Head*, lacked the immediacy of its predecessor. There were unprecedented changes of tempo, abruptly clashing chord sequences and far more understated melodies, often bordering on the bland. Or so it seemed. Like Radiohead's *OK Computer,* however, this was not a record that could be fully appreciated on first hearing. Only over time and with the benefit of repeated listening did it become apparent that Coldplay had comfortably surpassed their own not inconsiderable efforts on *Parachutes* and delivered a classic album of the modern era.

The juddering tempo of mournful album opener, 'Politik', was a clear sign that this new album was not going to be as easy a ride as its predecessor. Whereas *Parachutes* had seduced the listener from the outset with the gentle strumming of 'Don't Panic', 'Politik' crashed in with an almost military, big-gun drum line, spliced with clanging guitars and overwhelming massed, sustained violins, the nearest thing to a wall of sound that Coldplay have thus far produced. Chris uses his acutely controlled falsetto to great effect as ever, in contrast to the hammering insistence of the musical backdrop. The usual Coldplay dynamics are present, though, a reminder that this was the same band, with the characteristic drop from the pulsing thunder of the intro/chorus to trembling-vocal-and-chiming-piano-only verses. After two towering choruses, Jon's sparingly phrased guitar brushes on the bridge take the song onto an ever-escalating maelstrom that climaxes in truly epic style. A shuddering, shocking and exquisite start.

Next up was 'In My Place', the track that may have saved Coldplay from an early grave and an obvious lead single from the album. When it was released in August 2002, it stalled at number two, kept off the top spot by *Pop Idol*'s persistent king of reality cheese, Darius Danesh. However, the song announced loudly that Coldplay were back.

Without question it's Jon's finest guitar riff to date, reminding the listener of a cross between The Edge and the Bunnymen's Will Sergeant. Reassuringly cosy, it is one of the few songs on the record that becomes familiar after only one listen. Opening with the hi-hat high in the mix, followed by the guitar riff, the track then falls back into the drum/bass/vocal and soft organ tones of the verse. The drums strain at the leash each time the chorus and *that* riff come round again.

After the more expansive lyrics of 'Politik', 'In My Place' brings Chris back to more familiar, bittersweet territory of regret and confessional melancholy. The mix of the anthemic and the infectious made for a potent opening single and must have had the record executives rubbing their hands together with glee. That this song was a throwback from the *Parachutes* sessions was demonstrably obvious, but it was done with such finesse that this mattered little. Had the band delivered an album's worth of this material, which has such clear genealogical reference points in both 'Trouble' and 'Yellow', then they might have struggled to eclipse their first album. But as the next nine songs showed, this second album was very much more than just *Parachutes Mk II*.

The shadow of Ian McCulloch over the album sessions made its first clear mark on the third track, 'God Put A Smile Upon Your Face'. You could almost mistake Chris's vocal for that of Ian, particularly on this song's enormous chorus. Even the lyrics, with their pseudo-religious references and epic flavour, could have been taken directly from the Bunnymen songbook. It seems likely, too, that Coldplay have been influenced by singer Stephen Jones, formerly of Babybird, one of the UK's most under-rated yet gifted writers.

'God Put A Smile…' was completed during the initial sessions before moving to Parr Street, but the band was not happy with the end result. Guy was concerned his bass line was too mechanical and inappropriate, so he and Chris sat down to work through and solve the problem. In the end, they wrote a new bass line, opting for a bouncy groove to fire the song along with an uplifting tempo. That was all it took and the song was now complete; prior to this, the track was going to be dropped from the record altogether – now it was one of the band's favourites. There's a whiff of the blues in the finished track though the vocal, for once, falls a little short of the usual high standard, not in delivery, but in the rather uninteresting melody. The closing bars reek of Ian McCulloch again, although there are also snippets of those other Liverpool bands, The La's and their later mutation, Cast.

Next up was another highlight, future second single 'The Scientist'. When this was written, Coldplay had about eight songs shaping up for the album in one form or another. Jon and Chris caught the train to Liverpool and reviewed the material completed so far, which led them to start messing about with an old, out-of-tune piano. Chris had been listening to 'All Things Must Pass' by George Harrison and liked the swirling chord sequence, so tried to replicate it while mucking about on this piano. Suddenly the main chord sequence of 'The Scientist' presented itself and they both looked at each other, knowing they had come across something special. They worked on it excitedly and it was completed there and then, with the actual vocal and piano on the mastered track identical to the one they created that day. Chris later recalled, in a brilliant interview for *ShakenStir* internet magazine, how, "The best moment of the entire record for me was when we came back to this song, that's my favourite bit on the record. That was a great moment because it was brilliant."

Opening with one of Chris's by-now trademark piano lines, elegiac, painfully sad and utterly hypnotising, the song plunges deep into his fragile inner world of relationships. His emotions are brought sharply into focus for this track, with an unashamed and endearing honesty to his regretful, apologetic lyrics, which rue the end of what remains an obviously deeply cherished love. Yet another Coldplay song that could be as impressive with just a piano and a voice, the gradual build-up of acoustic strumming, strings and clean, pragmatic bass works perfectly. As with 'Yellow', this track displays a rare ability to present a highly sophisticated song and idea in a form that seems almost childlike in its simplicity.

As the second single from the new album, 'The Scientist' was complemented by an awesome video shot between September 30 and October 3 in Surrey and London, directed by Jamie Thraves, the man behind the videos for Goldie's 'Temper, Temper' and The Verve's 'Lucky Man'. Filmed entirely in reverse (in reference to the lyrics of "going back to the start"), Chris had to first learn the whole song backwards. The disturbing clip shows Chris and his on-screen girlfriend in the immediate aftermath of a car crash, with her apparently lifeless body lying in a field. Chris wakes up from the impact still strapped into his seat, and as he runs away from the tragedy, it becomes apparent that his girl removed her seatbelt momentarily before the crash in order to take off her coat. At that split second, a lorry loses control in front of them, destroying them both, her physically and him emotionally.

Viewed alongside the neon brightness and day-glo world of MTV and the modern pop video, it is a deeply distressing clip, on a par with Radiohead's paean to suicide and rat-race self-loathing, 'No Surprises', with its devastating head-only single-take video of Thom Yorke being gradually immersed in water (Thraves had worked with Radiohead too). Later in 2005, the video was voted the 11th greatest of all-time in Channel 4's list of the best 100 promo clips.

'Clocks', the third single from the album, hit number nine in the singles chart in March, 2003; for the B-side, Ash's Tim Wheeler played guitar on '1.36' and Simon Pegg, the comedian-turned-film-star, provided backing vocals on the same track. Another rushing piano line leads into a tumbling melody, which prefaces yet another stabbing drum track, although not quite as staccato as on 'Politik'. Curiously, this was the last track to make it on to the album, yet it seems impossible to imagine the record without it. The band had almost left 'Clocks' off *A Rush Of Blood To The Head* because they'd already captured 10 songs and were ready to can the sessions, when Chris walked in late one night and played them a rough version on piano. Talking to the *Cleveland Plain Dealer*, Chris revealed that, "The riff just came out, and

I showed it to Jonny and he wrote these cool chords underneath it, and we had a song that was mega." Assuming they had missed the chance to include it on this album, they placed the track on a new demo marked up as 'Songs for #3', namely for the next album. The credit for its inclusion must go to the 'fifth member' of the band, Phil Harvey (note how Harvey is listed in the liner notes for the second album with the rest of the band, not under management or the acknowledgements). He was convinced that the omission of the song was a mistake and insisted that the band look at it again. The problem was that the bare bones of the track were not working at this stage. Phil implored them to look at the music afresh and with great results: first the guitar chords, then the charging bass and finally the crashing drums suddenly fell together. The complex arrangement and accelerating climax are all handled with just the right amount of understatement. This is a fine example of the rest of the band knowing more about what to leave out than what to add, leaving the undoubted centrifuge that is Chris Martin to shine.

More chaotic and abrasive than the material on the previous album, 'Clocks' indicates that it is unwise to write off Coldplay as mere balladeers. The hint of McCulloch lurking in the corner of the studio is undeniable, particularly 'The Cutter'-era Bunnymen, but this is definitely all Coldplay.

Yet more abrupt military-style drums abound on the oddity that is 'Daylight'. Mixing decidedly Eastern guitar motifs also reminiscent of 'The Cutter' with melancholy vocals and baritone backing vocals, this is a peculiar yet captivating number. Guy's bass is at its most agile although the uplifting chorus and falsetto vocal are a bit harsh on the ear.

The Eastern feel comes courtesy of a 12-string guitar played with a slide, in a similar way to that which ex-Beatle George Harrison made all his own. The track was captured on tape very quickly, an approach that the otherwise perfectionist band positively pursued: 'We've been quite lucky," said Chris, "that we've recorded a lot of stuff down as soon as it's been written because you spend most of your life trying to recreate those first moments." In this way, the band played back a tape of the piano and vocal, played along to it and, subject to some clever loops and programming, that was that.

On first hearing, it seems as if the album is about to tail off, that the band's muse is spent, but fortunately they are confident enough to kick back from the sharpness of 'Daylight' and deliver the gentle, Lemonheads-esque 'Green Eyes'. For once a song about an apparently successful relationship, this jaunty tune features unadorned instrumentation, limited effects (save mainly for some vocal echo) and minimal backing. Said to be a direct result of Guy's growing love for country & western music, it reflects the band's growing confidence that they even saw fit to attempt such a chirpy number. Comically, Guy may have inspired the track but he was said to like the finished article least of all. This romantic track (along with album closer, 'Amsterdam') was recorded with the minimum of fuss and provides a perfect counterpoint to the epic likes of 'Clocks' and 'Politik'. A product of the original but largely aborted sessions, they returned to 'Green Eyes' four months later, mixed the tapes and it was done. Interestingly, the end of the song was written in Iceland, which Chris says is "the perfect place to write music".

The romantic flavour continues unabated with the openly sentimental 'Warning Sign'. Despite detailing a failed relationship and the part played in that by the singer's mistakes, the feelings still obviously burn strongly and it is hard not to hope there is room for a reconciliation. For once, Chris makes no secret of the fact that this is a song of deep regret about the break-up with his girlfriend, 26-year-old radio executive Lily Sobhani, at the time of promoting *Parachutes*. They had been dating for a year, just before the band really started to take off, and Chris had even started thinking of buying a ring and proposing.

'Warning Sign' was an old song that Chris did not originally want on the album, but he was outvoted by the rest of the band who were insistent that its touching tones be included. Oddly, he says that the song makes the listener feel sorry for the singer when in fact he was, in his opinion, behaving like an idiot at the time. This mid-tempo, shuffling ballad is the result and here, rather than the guitars, it is Chris's yearning vocal line on the chorus that is the hook. Embellished with sumptuous strings and nursery school-percussion, this is a warm, charming song, reminiscent of Lloyd Cole. The false ending with sparse piano and soft strings appears to close the song, only for it to continue for nearly another minute and a half with Chris's increasingly wavering vocals and imploring lyrics. It captures the sense of unfinished emotional business that the lyrics describe.

A rare lapse comes next in the rather dull 'A Whisper'. Too overtly referential to the Bunnymen, this track is easily the album's weakest moment; the band later admitted that Macca had asked them if they had a song on the album that was 3/4 timing – they hadn't, so this was included. The vocal is too low in the mix, probably quite deliberately so, but nonetheless with the result that the top end just blurs it out, rather than sealing it as a whisper. The chiming guitars are too much a pastiche of early U2 circa *War/Boy* and the overall effect is disappointingly tame, rather like a derivative Sixties film soundtrack.

The penultimate song, the title track, with its haunting Pink Floyd-esque warblings, returns to more familiar territory (although it is hard to avoid the comparisons to Radiohead's 'Exit Music (From A Film)'). Sounding not unlike a Western soundtrack, it is yet another ruthlessly simple song and production. Centring around impulsiveness, it seems to summarise the tone of the entire album. Again sounding like Stephen Jones at his finest, the vocals are almost spoken-word, until Chris screams into the chorus where Jon's stabbing guitar riffs accompany him back to the next gentle verse, at the beginning of which a slither of backing vocal from Chris sounds a lot like Bono. The country & western twang reappears with the string-bending lead guitar, but the galloping drums and driving bass keep it firmly in rock territory.

The closing track is an atmospheric lament called 'Amsterdam', which in some ways reverts to type, but isn't a formulaic song by any means. The doleful piano and swooping vocals coalesce with refined precision, ably assisted by subtle backing harmonies, while the absence of excessive instrumentation lulls the listener into a becalmed sense of mellowness. Then, in a perfect example of the newly mature Coldplay, the song's entire solemnity is abruptly crushed beneath the weight of a crashing onslaught of sound. Like 'Green Eyes' before it, this song was a relatively easy one to write and was recorded pretty much live. Few bands can boast such dynamics, few think to try and even fewer can carry it off.

Overall, the album was a clear progression from *Parachutes,* yet the technology used was essentially the same. The bigger sound was doubtless necessary for the band to avoid the often problematic task of playing so many mellow songs on increasingly bigger live stages. Yet, it wasn't just a case of using more instruments and playing louder: they had all evolved immensely as players and soaked up many influences on their world travels.

Chris made the new album sound all the more enticing when he revealed to VH1 some of the personal events that had surrounded its writing (virtually all of which the band kept a closely guarded secret): "[It's] born from all the places we've been and the things we've experienced. Some of our friends have died and some of us have fallen in love. Some of us have fallen out of love and some of us have been to Haiti and some us have been to Australia. Some of us have met Bono and some of us have met someone with nothing. It's like a massive culture gun fired at our heads. All this stuff has been happening to us, and now we have the opportunity to put it into some songs." That said, at a time when so much of music was obsessed with blending as many genres as possible into each album or even a single song, it was refreshing to hear something so focused, and so proudly ignorant of current fashion.

Coldplay had surpassed *Parachutes* and then some. What appeared at first as a possibly unwieldy and complex record was on further investigation a sophisticated, lush and elegantly produced masterpiece. Certainly the record against which all others of 2002 would be judged. Chris had hinted that he was aiming to match his own favourite albums, particularly Radiohead's *The Bends* and U2's *The Unforgettable Fire*.

The fact that *A Rush Of Blood To The Head* was more of an acquired taste than *Parachutes* somehow added to the record's (and by association the band's) allure. The knowledge that they had found the recording experience so painstaking fuelled the feeling that this was a record of rare complexity. The tales of possible splits and personal arguments exaggerated the sense that this record needed to be savoured and enjoyed *just in case* those "final album" rumours proved to be true. Intentionally or not, the rumour mill swirling around the album had only enhanced its value. The only possible reservation was whether the more demanding atmosphere and depth would strike a chord with a public increasingly fed on a diet of reality TV pop and homogenised chart fodder?

The simple answer was a resounding yes! In the UK, the new album easily took the number one slot on its release. First week sales were 250,000, nearly five times that of the first album. This was matched by a number one slot in many other countries around the world. Early sales figures suggested that the near-2,000,000 mark achieved in the UK by *Parachutes* was quickly under serious threat. America seemed ready to embrace Coldplay also, a very promising sign indeed – across the Atlantic, the album went in the *Billboard* charts at an amazingly high number five.

What was very striking about *A Rush…* was the level of critical acclaim, which surpassed even the gushing reviews given to *Parachutes*. *Amazon.com* praised "a soulful, exhilarating journey, without once breaking its mesmerizing spell… the music is nearly flawless. This is exquisite stuff." *The Guardian's* Alex Petridis wrote: "You feel you already know and like these songs the first time you hear them. The last band to pull off this remarkable feat was Oasis… it is all down to beautifully crafted songwriting and an all-pervading aura of warm inclusiveness." Remember this journalist's less than complimentary review of *Parachutes*? Yet for all this new enthusiasm, Petridis did have some complaints: "There is no mystery here. Whatever *A Rush of Blood To The Head* has to offer is apparent straight away. It is finely wrought and brilliantly realised, but devoid of charming idiosyncrasy. It is comfortable rather than challenging, varied without being devastatingly original."

However, this was a rare voice of dissent. Almost universally, the album was received as a modern classic. Even the artwork was revered. Several years later, in 2010, the Royal Mail would release a series of stamps of classic album covers and Coldplay's *A Rush Of Blood To The Head* was chosen alongside records by Pink Floyd, Blur, The Clash, Led Zeppelin, The Rolling Stones, New Order, Primal Scream, David Bowie and Mike Oldfield. The artwork would also later be included in an exhibition at London's Barbican Art Gallery called 'Communicate: Independent British Graphic Design Since The Sixties' alongside such seminal album covers, posters campaigns and pop videos as The Beatles' *Sgt Pepper's Lonely Hearts Club Band*, Massive Attack's *Mezzanine*, Jamie Reid's designs for The Sex Pistols and Peter Saville's work for Factory Records, Joy Division and Suede.

Back in 2002/3, however, all the band had to do now was tour the record to every territory that had bought into the project, which at that time looked pretty much like every record-buying country on earth. One notable non-commercial aside was that as a sign of their ambition to be as consistent as possible with their message, for *A Rush Of Blood To The Head* the band calculated the greenhouse gas emissions created by manufacturing and distributing such a global corporate product. By way of ecological recompense, they bought 10,000 mango trees for villages in India, with the help of the British firm Carbon Neutral Co.

Before setting off on a mammoth world trek, Chris had a few suitably unpredictable words to say about the record himself: "I can never listen to anything we do once it's finished because there's always something that isn't really finished… you just flick through the tracks, one by one by one really quickly and it sounds like another album by another band of just 11 songs. And yet to us it's weeks, months, years of work."

Ahead of them was even more work. Parlophone installed them as its worldwide priority for 2002/3. This privileged position was helped by the fact that the parent company EMI's other big acts – Kylie, Geri and Radiohead – did not have new records to promote. With the album in the charts, the critics in a lather and the full backing of the record company across the globe, stadium status for Coldplay seemed only a matter of time.

At the end of August, 2002, Coldplay returned to the UK after their lengthy spell overseas for a triumphant one-off homecoming gig at London's Kentish Town Forum, the same week that *A Rush…* was heading for number one in the album charts. The last time the band would cram their by-now colossal following into a 2,000-capacity venue prior to their forthcoming arena tour, the gig was one of the band's most special live shows to date.

The material on the new album demanded a more epic sound. For the older songs from the début album, tracks like 'Yellow' and 'Trouble', as well as recent single 'In My Place', the devoted crowd sang the entire choruses (prompting Chris to shout "We've finally made it to stadium rock!"). In a self-mocking dig at their failure to beat *Pop Idol* comeback king Darius Danesh to the number one single spot with 'In My Place', Chris dedicated 'Trouble' to the lanky Scots pop oddity, saying, "Darius is more handsome!"

Introduced by Steve Lamacq as the show was being broadcast live on BBC Radio 1, the gig was a storming set. Again the crowd was crammed with celebrities, including Dave Grohl of Foo Fighters, The Cooper Temple Clause, Sean Hughes and Ash (Coldplay performed a cover of the latter's 'Shining Light'). They also played 'Flying Without Wings' by Westlife, a band they openly disliked, plus a rendition of 'Happy Birthday' for manager Phil Harvey. All in all, it was a memorable night, probably more so for the band than for the ecstatic audience. Here they were, three years after their first gig, playing to a rapturous 2,000-strong crowd as a 'small' show, having sold five million albums and returned triumphant from a fawning USA. "This is the most fun I've ever had in my life!" barked a delirious Chris Martin.

The international campaign got off to an inauspicious start when the band realised that many outside of the UK did not understand what the album's title phrase actually meant. Some Japanese journalists kept asking them if they were blushing with embarrassment at the record! But this was a minor hiccup in what proved to be an outstanding world tour for Coldplay. Before flying out to the US, the band played an impromptu secret gig at north London's tiny Shepherd's Pub in Highgate. Not even a single employee at their record label, Parlophone, knew about it. Guy was absent with a cold, but the remaining trio still managed to work through a handful of their own songs plus some bizarre covers, including Bon Jovi's 'Livin' On A Prayer', 'Sweet Child O' Mine' by Guns N' Roses, The Sex Pistols' 'Pretty Vacant', T Rex's '20th Century Boy' as well as their usual rendition of Nancy Sinatra's Bond theme, 'You Only Live Twice'. After the set, Chris asked punters to donate money for Whittington Hospital, the birthplace of guitarist Jon Buckland (this raised £300). Despite these odd choices, the band's most peculiar cover has to be the one they played during a late 2002 tour of Europe, when they shocked their Copenhagen crowd by copying the bubblegum pop masterpiece/horror-show 'Barbie Girl' by Scandinavia's Aqua. Chris took the role of Barbie and Jon played the part of her boyfriend, Ken. The cover only lasted one minute because the pair fell about laughing and could not continue.

Most impressively of all during this period was Coldplay's monumental progress in America. With Nettwerk Records expertly pushing the album for all its worth, they found their face on billboards all across the States as well as on hefty and exorbitantly expensive in-store merchandising and full-page adverts in newspapers. Journalist Tracey Pepper from influential US music magazine *Spin* made no secret of the fact that the band were perfectly placed to take America by storm: "The music industry here is excited because they were one of the only non-rap/metal 'rock' bands to have a bona fide hit. Chris has become a truly engaging frontman. They're vastly improved live. They're also willing to put in the time touring. Breaking America is not a right. It takes a lot of work."

The initial three-week push in the USA saw them playing sizeable venues in key cities such as Chicago, New York and Los Angeles. Not for the first time did the band find themselves with many high-profile celebrities in the audience but it was the frenetic nature of the audience's reaction that was so encouraging this time around.

The coming year would take them home for an arena-sized UK tour (supported by the magnificent Idlewild), back to America several times, numerous festival headline slots, Japan and provisionally Australasia too. The arena tour in the UK was final proof – if any was needed – that Coldplay were now one of their home country's biggest acts. The sellout dates included two nights at Wembley Arena, which reputedly could have sold out five times over. The material from their two albums was complemented by occasional covers of the Bunnymen's 'Lips Like Sugar' and Bowie's 'Heroes'.

Nevertheless, the live shows attracted their share of bad reviews too. Maybe it was the mellow nature of so much of their material that failed to sit well in the increasingly large arenas they were playing. Maybe Chris's lack of confidence was still evident. Whatever the reason, unlike their almost universally applauded recorded output, Coldplay's live shows have received some negative coverage such as this piece in *The Brain*

Farm magazine: "To my ears, they still don't have enough tunes to cut it live ... after a while the tunes did seem to blend into each other. 'Sparks' drags on and on, so does 'We Never Change'. A few others work, but it's all [too] relentlessly one-paced to make a real impact. At the moment, they're still finding their feet."

CHAPTER 14

Going Round The Bends

The Top 5 placing of *A Rush...* in the *Billboard* charts was no doubt helped by the success of Radiohead's awkward recent album *Kid A* and their previous smash hit, *OK Computer*. The Oxford-based band and Coldplay have often been compared to one another, and it is worth dwelling on the similarities a little further.

Like Coldplay, Thom Yorke's outfit also met at an educational establishment, albeit much earlier – Thom met bassist Colin Greenwood at secondary school aged only 14. The speed of the band's progress was much slower than Coldplay's too – it wasn't until five years later that Radiohead's line-up solidified and they played their first gig at the Jericho Tavern in their hometown. Whereas Coldplay "borrowed" their name, Radiohead started off with the rather amateur-sounding On A Friday, but thankfully changed this soon after, albeit taking the moniker from a strange reggae track on Talking Heads' *True Stories* album. Instead of a friend managing them, their pal handed the tape to former musician Chris Hufford at a local studio who promptly took on the role of manager, a task he has fulfilled with stunning brilliance.

Like Coldplay, Radiohead signed to EMI after numerous gigs and much record-label interest, although the latter signed their deal after only recording a demo, not with the benefit of actual independent releases as with Coldplay. Radiohead's March 1992 *Drill EP* charted at number 101, even lower than Coldplay's 'Brothers & Sisters', and likewise prompted the Oxford band to look for new producers (their manager, Hufford, had produced the EP).

Unlike Coldplay, Radiohead's début album was completed in just three weeks. Unlike Coldplay, it did not reach number one nor did it turn the band into megastars almost overnight. However, like Coldplay, it did contain Radiohead's own 'Yellow'. The track was called 'Creep' but it failed to attract either the sales or critical acclaim of Coldplay's 'Yellow'. Instead the 6,000 UK sales of the single (getting it to number 78 rather than number five for 'Yellow') and modest reviews suggested Radiohead would only ever be moderate achievers. However, like 'Yellow', the single became a huge radio smash in the US and this turned everything around for Radiohead. And like 'Yellow', 'Creep' brought such unexpected pressure on Radiohead that for a while there was a very real chance that the band would never make it intact to the second album.

It was just as well they did, because unlike Coldplay, Radiohead's début album, *Pablo Honey*, was simply not strong enough to turn them into one of the world's biggest bands. The protracted tour that the success of 'Creep' forced the band to undertake left them, like Chris Martin, bereft of time and inspiration for new material. When the second album sessions started, morale was pitifully low and there was genuine concern for the band's survival. After some aborted sessions, the band toured Down Under before returning, energised, to complete the album in two weeks.

While Coldplay were allowed no time to grow up in public, being thrust into such an intense spotlight with their very first album, Radiohead waited until their sophomore effort to make that break. The record was called *The Bends* and for Radiohead it changed *everything*.

Instead of being seen as a whimsical, sometimes odd pop/rock band, *The Bends* revealed the far deeper and more complex songwriting genius that was at work within Radiohead. It particularly showcased Thom Yorke and enigmatic guitarist Johnny Greenwood's talents.

Although an album behind Coldplay (in terms of critical success), Radiohead were now seen as very genuine contenders in the world of rock and like the former were quickly filling larger venues across the world.

Unlike Coldplay, it wasn't until a later single from the album, 'Street Spirit (Fade Out)', that the public really caught on to the band. While Coldplay have enjoyed a profile almost from their very first major release, Radiohead were finally reaping the rewards of years and years of hard work.

The musical comparison with Coldplay really comes to the fore with this understated and quite beautiful second Radiohead album. However, their third album, the epochal *OK Computer* – now regularly highly placed on any 'Best Album Ever' list – sees Radiohead begin to mark out their territory as one of the world's most experimental and unique bands. While songs such as 'Clocks' and 'Politik' do remind the listener of much of this third Radiohead album, particularly the crashing climaxes and crescendos of noise, there are far more reference points to *A Rush...* than just these two Radiohead albums.

Also, Coldplay had yet to make a habit of writing songs that lasted eight minutes or longer. Coldplay also had the pressure of a deadline for their second album while Radiohead were told to hand in the third album only when they were ready. On a more superficial note, Chris even wears an elastic bandage on his wrist when playing the guitar, because of repetitive strain pains, but obviously this leads to inevitable comparisons with the contraption worn by Johnny Greenwood.

Radiohead have enjoyed similar critical acclaim to Coldplay, sharing numerous awards including a Grammy for 'Best Alternative Album'. Much of their attention focuses on singer Thom Yorke, who is a shy, elusive and peculiarly brilliant frontman. Coldplay's Jon Buckland is admired by many for his individuality and idiosyncratic experimentalism – likewise Radiohead guitarist Johnny Greenwood.

Both bands regularly express their disdain at press intrusion and acknowledge the absurdity of their job and position. Both bands' videos are also acclaimed – the similarities between the impact of the promo clips for 'The Scientist' and 'No Surprises' has already been discussed.

Both bands also support various charities such as Amnesty International, Make Trade Fair and numerous children's charities.

Like Coldplay, Radiohead fiercely control every aspect of their career. They design the artwork themselves although it has to be said it is far more obscure and at times pretentious than the sleeves for *Parachutes* and *A Rush...* Like Coldplay, Radiohead enjoy huge success in America, at this point in their respective careers far more so than Chris Martin's outfit. *OK Computer* was a number one album in America and the band already played stadiums over there, a benchmark Coldplay were yet to reach.

Nonetheless, it always seemed unlikely that Coldplay would follow Radiohead's footsteps and veer off into the deeply peculiar vein of avante-garde music that saw them produce the aesthetically uncommercial but critically acclaimed albums *Kid A* (another US number one and another Grammy winner) and *Amnesiac*. Certainly there had been signs from Coldplay's second album that the band were not happy to deliver simple three-minute ballads ad infinitum. Yet it is Radiohead's instinct to hurtle into such unorthodox waters that has opened up the vacuum for a new melancholy guitar band that Coldplay are perfectly suited to fill.

One final point about all this musical semantics. To be fair, bands so often moan about comparisons being made and, worse still, come out with phrases such as "our music isn't really like anyone else's" or "don't pigeonhole us", but they misinterpret the intentions of the magazines who do this. After all, these magazine writers are bombarded with hundreds of new bands each year and have to describe and translate to their readers what each one sounds like. Without referring to other bands, this would be virtually impossible.

The problem is exacerbated by the fact that bands become overly precious about it all. Coldplay are probably wise to try to avoid this pigeonhole – as mentioned it can sometimes prove suffocating – but ultimately they will be judged by their own musical output and if that is not good enough, then no amount of positive comparisons with any band will save them.

As a final note on the subject, when Chris eventually came across Radiohead's frontman, the occasion was a huge disappointment, as he told *Entertainment Weekly*: "Thom Yorke ignored me at a hotel in Los Angeles. I was secretly a bit gutted. I'm sure he recognised me. I always look at it like we're in a big musical high school and Radiohead is in the year above us and they still haven't come and sat with us at lunch."

CHAPTER 15

Sneaking In Through The (Sliding) Doors

Coldplay's success has inevitably brought about a relentless media interest in their private lives, particularly that of Chris Martin. Of specific fascination at this point in their exploding career was Chris's relationship with beautiful Hollywood actress Gwyneth Paltrow. Famed for a notoriously tearful Oscar acceptance speech, Gwyneth has inadvertently introduced the new millennial term of "doing a Gwyneth" into the lexicon. New York-raised Paltrow is five years Chris's senior, close friends with Madonna and the McCartney daughters and mixes in the very highest echelons of the Hollywood A-list jet set. So how did this seemingly bizarre coupling come about?

Gwyneth was first spotted at US Coldplay shows in early 2001, but it seems it wasn't until the show at New York's Bowery Ballroom in autumn 2002 that the pair actually met on more personal terms. Since then it was suggested that Gwyneth went to every US gig as well as both the Brits and Grammys.

At first, Chris laughed off suggestions of an affair. He said that if he stood next to comedian Les Dennis, the paparazzi would be interested only in photos of the latter. He pointed out that he was also supposed to be dating Natalie Imbruglia. "It's really mad, fame. Should I sue them? I was really pissed off with them because it's not true. The only person I've ever been pictured embracing in public was Mo Mowlam and I'm fine with that." Another rumoured relationship with the quirky Nelly Furtado was apparently over as soon as it had (allegedly) started. Again this was strenuously denied and ultimately proved to be nothing more than fiction.

Previously Chris's relationships had been very low profile, even soliciting the man himself to admit he was "a loser in all things romantic", with some of the less than sensitive tabloids pointing out this "self-confessed nerd" had only lost his virginity aged 22 (he had mentioned this to a journalist, regretted it immediately and asked for it not to be printed). This admission in the music press was a small slip-up but it was magnified a thousandfold when *The Sun* splashed the story across its 'showbiz' pages the following week.

Gwyneth, of course, was no stranger to the world of tabloid journalism. Only recently she had expressed shock at discovering the paparazzi rifling through her garbage, claiming paper shredders had been invented "for girls like me". She had also ironically just declared that British men never asked her out. Although she later seemed to retract this statement, claiming she had been misquoted, it made it seem all the more peculiar that she was now purported to be dating Chris Martin, a quiet, shy Englishman. Naturally, she wouldn't commit, saying, "I don't read any newspaper that has any gossip in it. I read *The Financial Times*. I don't really know what [the tabloids] think and what they say."

Nonetheless, the next thing Coldplay fans saw were pictures of Chris running from a car, hunched under increasingly large woolly hats, into Gwyneth's London home. Tabloid bibles such as *Heat* tagged onto the latest celebrity couple like a magnet. With Posh and Becks keeping a low profile after the horrific kidnap threats against Victoria Beckham and their children, plus Justin Timberlake and Britney Spears having split, not everyone wanted to read about Michael Douglas and Catherine Zeta-Jones suing *OK!* for £1 million. Ever hungry, the spotlight scanned elsewhere in celebrity land and, alighting on Gwyneth's beauty and Chris's current acclaim, elevated the pair to the level where a trip to the supermarket became front-page news. It seemed that at first even Chris couldn't help notice the apparent incongruity of the match: "She's a big Hollywood star and I'm just the bloke from Coldplay."

But this was hardly a real life *Notting Hill*. The extent of Coldplay's critical adulation had extended into the realm of celebrity applause too, not least with the band's ever-growing guest list of superstars. Chris was also beginning a winning streak of 'World's Sexiest Man' awards. So this was not exactly a beauty and the beast; no Monroe and Miller. There were other reasons to suggest the relationship was entirely plausible too. Both were known for their clean-living and both had enjoyed somewhat privileged upbringings. Also, Gwyneth made no secret of the fact she found much of her celebrity life nauseating. Gwyneth was still reeling from the loss of her father from throat cancer in 2001 and it seemed that this new relationship had really taken her by welcome surprise. She made no secret of the fact that, unsurprisingly, when her beloved father died she was emotionally bereft. She said she had lost her sense of humour and struggled to enjoy what to many would have appeared to have been a fulfilling life. However, meeting Chris and starting a relationship with him was the perfect fillip and she spoke of how he had helped her get her "spark" back.

By October 2002, the veil of secrecy surrounding their relationship seemed to have slipped away. At Coldplay's second Wembley Arena show in that month, midway through their encore, Chris dedicated 'In My Place' to Gwyneth. He didn't say he was her boyfriend, and he also dedicated several songs to his mother who was in the crowd, but this was nonetheless a recognition that a relationship of sorts existed. This was fuelled when Gwyneth was also spotted at the Dublin show of this same set of dates.

By the start of November 2002, UK tabloids had squeezed more snippets out of Chris. He admitted to having been on dates with Gwyneth but denied that they were yet an item. In a eulogy that must have had Alan McGee steaming at the ears, he said to *The Sun*, "I'm proud to be with someone who's very nice and very beautiful but she's not my girlfriend at the moment. I feel out of my depth with all this. I met her for the first time at our gig at Wembley... it's early days. I got her number, rang her and asked if she wanted to meet. We went out at the weekend and we seem to get on... I don't know when we're going out again. I feel uncomfortable talking about her. We're just becoming friends."

Despite this understandable reluctance to talk and his clear wish to keep his private life exactly that – private – by now the rumour mill was in full operation. Gwyneth was reported to be so smitten with Chris that she flew her mother, Blythe Danner, to a party at Sting and wife Trudie Styler's house just to meet her new beau. *Heat* magazine even went as far as to get bookies odds of 2-1 on the Paltrow/Martin pairing as "favourite celebrity couple to get married this year". Others made comparisons to Madonna and Guy Ritchie, a similar duo of public-school educated Brit and high-profile US star.

Despite having been dating only four months, the pair spent Christmas and New Year's Eve together at the Martin family home in Devon, a splendid 19th century manor house. In a scene straight out of pretty much any Hugh Grant film, Chris was even seen buying Ms Paltrow a pint at his local pub, The Royal Oak in Nadderwater ('Good Food, Fine Ales'). Not exactly The Ivy, but Gwyneth seemed not to care. Nor did she mind going to see Chris's 11-year-old sister in panto.

Switching continents, the pair flew to Los Angeles for the New Year with Gwyneth's mother, albeit after checking in separately to avoid prying eyes. Despite such subterfuge, Chris's guitar case was clearly spotted on Gwyneth's luggage trolley so the cover-up was rather unconvincing.

Then of course, according to the press, who seemed unduly pleased, it was all over. Six months after the news had started to break of a relationship, the February 2003 tabloids announced Gwyneth had ended the affair. Reports suggested that her previously troubled love life had left her determined not to be dumped and have her heart broken again – having seen former boyfriends Ben Affleck and Brad Pitt both end their relationships with her first. Unnamed "friends" said she had "toughened up" and that she only ever saw Chris as "an in-between lover". Other anonymous sources suggested that Chris was "happy being single before he met Gwyneth, but she really has cast a spell on him and he seems ready to settle down." These rumours of a split were never substantiated.

Chris kept a dignified silence during much of this but did offer a few snippets of altogether confusing thoughts. At the *NME* Awards ceremony he told the press pack that "I am dating Julia Roberts" while another reporter who asked him about Paltrow was informed, "I don't know the girl, I've never even met her."

No one seemed quite certain if the affair was indeed over for a while but then magazines started running features again, such as 'Sizzling Snoggin' Snaps'. Gwyneth was said to have moved into Chris's north London flat; Chris was seen affectionately hugging her on set of her new movie, *Ted And Sylvia*; they spent the entire Valentine weekend together and, again only rumour, they were said to be attending the Oscars together. In the event, they didn't but only because the Oscar ceremony was deliberately subdued in light of the war with Iraq. For once the tabloids had something really important to splash on their front pages.

Bizarrely, the juggernaut of Coldplay's success that followed the release of *A Rush Of Blood To The Head* was by now so weighty that reporters were asking Gwyneth if *she* felt insecure in the relationship, bearing in mind Chris's newfound status as one of showbiz's premier men. By contrast, she remained very cagey about Chris when pressed about children and the future: "I definitely don't feel ready to have [kids] right now. I love not working. I love sleeping late and just, you know, doing yoga and hanging out. It's just great."

On or off, engaged or not, the ultra-high profile of the Chris/Gwyneth relationship was final proof, if it was needed, of Coldplay's ascent – or perhaps descent - into celebrity hell. Perhaps only Chris was the man the paparazzi wanted to photograph – the other three band members' personal lives had up to this point remained almost completely private – but nonetheless, the band were now faced at every gig and appearance with flash bulbs and press scrums. The low profile of the other three band members was quite deliberate, as Will pointed out: "I don't feel famous at all. I like the way the name of the band is becoming more known, but I can put my hat on after a gig and slip into anonymity."

Will: "I don't feel famous at all. I like the way the name of the band is becoming more known, but I can put my hat on after a gig and slip into anonymity." The *MTV* Europe Music Awards in Barcelona, Spain. (JOHN ROGERS/GETTY IMAGES)

On stage with Noel Gallagher at an Oxfam charity gig, London Astoria, October 29, 2002. (TABATHA FIREMAN/REDFERNS)

The MTV Europe Music Awards, November 14, 2002. (ILPO MUSTO IM/LFI)

"Guy Berryman's a handsome bastard. He's responsible for all our calendar sales." (DAVE HOGAN/GETTY IMAGES)

Earls Court in 2005 and another 'shed' conquered. (BRIAN RASIC/REX FEATURES)

Headlining V Festival 2003, one of the '100 greatest gigs of all-time'. (BALKANPIX.COM/REX FEATURES)

A very modern rock star. (BRYCE DUFFY/CORBIS)

It's a long way from a cheap Japanese six-string aged 11. Jonny in 2001. (BRYCE DUFFY/CORBIS)

Globe-trotting in Sydney, Australia, 2006. (NEWSPIX/REX FEATURES)

Accepting another Brit award at Earls Court in 2006, while Madge looks on. (JOHN MARSHALL/LFI0)

The Hope For Haiti Now concert at The Hospital Club on January 22, 2010 in London. (DAVE M. BENETT/MTV VIA LFI)

Guy adds two more gongs for the band's mantelpiece at the *Q* Awards in 2008. (RICHARD YOUNG/REX FEATURES)

Viva La Coldplay! Live on stage in Belgium, November 4, 2004. (GOEDEFROIT MUSIC/LFI)

CHAPTER 16

When Will We Be Kings?

"I'm still getting used to seeing pictures of myself and hearing my voice on the radio, it's a strange thing to get used to. I am a pretty shy guy and I prefer to be anonymous. I love music but I never wanted to be a rock star."

Chris Martin

While the UK tabloids had obsessed about Chris and Gwyneth's closeness, the band were busy reinforcing their US profile. The dates in support of *A Rush...* certainly had their fair share of surprises. In September, 2002, determined to avoid a repeat of the earlier cancelled US gigs, the band were faced with yet another disaster after a freak wind storm blew the roof off a venue in Atlanta. Chris and Jon promptly set up in the venue's car park and played a surprise and avidly received mini-set to a delighted crowd. Ash, who was supporting Coldplay on these dates, also played an indoor replacement gig that night by way of further compensation. For their tracks 'Kung Fu' and 'Shining Light', Chris joined them on vocals.

In February, 2003, Coldplay announced that their next US gig would be the 20,000-seat Madison Square Garden, final confirmation that they were a serious player on the American music scene. This commercial success in the USA was complemented by the news that *A Rush...*

had been nominated for two Grammys, namely 'Best Alternative Music Album' and 'Best Rock Performance By Duo Or Group With Vocals' for the single 'In My Place'. Having flown by Concorde the night after the Brits to the ceremony, the 'Best Alternative Music Album' Grammy triumphantly went to Coldplay. On the night they performed live alongside other acts including Bruce Springsteen and Nelly (whose 'Hot In Herre' (sic) they had covered once in New York). America, it seemed, was theirs for the taking.

The campaign continued in January 2003 with a raft of yet more North American dates, 33 in total, which was extended well into March due to frenzied ticket demand. They then returned to Europe for 11 more shows, before flying to the UK for some arena dates in mid-April, at the *Manchester Evening News* Arena and the cavernous Earls Court in London. These three shows – their biggest indoor shows thus far in the UK – were preceded by their smallest, when they played a live session in front of just 30 people for BBC Radio 1's *Mark and Lard Show*. Then it was back out to America for yet more shows. The year of massive gigs – final confirmation if any was needed that Coldplay were now a stadium band – continued with news that they were to headline V2003 alongside Red Hot Chili Peppers. The V Festival gig was a classic, with sure signs that the band's many detractors were becoming a minority as the tens of thousands of fans sang along frantically to Coldplay's ever-growing set of classic songs. Twelve months later, in a special edition of Q magazine detailing 'The 100 Greatest Gigs Of All Time', this performance hit the lofty heights of number four, beaten only by the triumvirate of Oasis (Knebworth), Nirvana (Reading 1992) and the top draw, which was Radiohead at Glastonbury in 1997.

By March, 2003, they had already sold 4.5 million copies of *A Rush...*, a quite remarkable achievement. It was only a matter of time before these sales figures surged past those for *Parachutes*. There were even a few signs of new material, suggesting that this time around Chris was not finding writing as difficult as he had between the first and second albums. On the same day that 'The Scientist' entered the singles charts, Coldplay performed at The Royal Albert Hall in aid of the Teenage Cancer Trust, where two new songs were aired, namely 'Gravity' and a very rocky number called 'Marianne'. Unashamedly optimistic, after the triumphant V 2003 gig, Chris had told one reporter that the next Coldplay album would effectively "reinvent the wheel", a superficially ambitious comment that would in many ways haunt him for some time to come and hardly helped dilute the accusations from certain critical quarters that he was pompous.

In his brief moments away from the creative hub of Coldplay, Chris was also enjoying looking around at different musical experiences than just his main band. He had found time to record a duet with a favourite of his, Canadian singer-songwriter Ron Sexsmith. Their version of the country ballad 'Gold In Them Hills' was captured on tape at London's Electric Earth East Studios in mid-2002, and penned in to appear as a bonus track on Sexsmith's fifth album, *Cobblestone Runway*. Hardly the beginnings of a solo career, but certainly an intriguing diversion for fans and critics alike.

Although the two had previously appeared to get on, at the Teenage Cancer Trust show Oasis' Liam Gallagher took a direct swipe at both Chris and Gwyneth after the band made it known they were intensely anti-war. Liam took exception to what he felt was Chris using the event as a platform: "When Coldplay did this gig they banged on about the war, that's wrong. Chris Martin shouldn't be using this cause to bang on about his own views on the war. If him and his gawky bird want to go banging on about the war they can do it at their own gigs. That lot are just a bunch of knobhead students – Chris Martin looks like a geography teacher. What's all that with writing messages about Free Trade on his hand? If he wants to write things down I'll give him a pen and a pad of paper. Bunch of students. These gigs are about kids who have got cancer, they've got to fight a war every day of their lives. That's what we're all here doing this for." Despite this, many people in the crowd stood and applauded Chris when he encouraged them to "sing against the war."

The UK, of course, had already fallen. They played 'Clocks' on stage and dominated the February 2003 Brit Awards, most notably with 'Best Band' and 'Best Album' gongs, but the highlight of the night came when the camera panned over to where they were sitting to capture their reactions on hearing of yet another win, only to inexplicably find Chris on the stairway, posterior in the air and legs akimbo. He was on particularly good form and it seemed as though Coldplay and their enigmatic frontman had finally come to terms with what they represented and what that entailed. Will was openly extremely optimistic about the future, as he mused in *The Observer*: "We all found that first year in Coldplay, with all the success and acclaim and criticism, bewildering. We didn't lose it, but we lost our bearings, probably Chris most of all. Now we've got a handle on it and we're confident about who we are. We all feel very excited about what we can do. There are limitless possibilities."

Chris was equally much more at home with his role, both professionally and personally. This period marked the start of a definite change in his approach to the fame game, and from hereon he would become increasingly self-deprecating, humourous and constantly looking to have a laugh. Given the previous accusations of being 'earnest' this was a welcome development. One specific example during these busy months was a midnight record-store opening to buy signed copies of David Gray's new album, the appropriately named *New Day At Midnight*. Chris turned up at the last minute and asked to buy five copies. When staff recognised him, they offered him free copies but he insisted on paying. When they refused his money, he gave them the equivalent amount of cash to go and buy some drinks for themselves instead.

Critics can be quick to denigrate rock stars for finding their fame a strange bedfellow but consider this: in the spring of 1999, Chris Martin was an aspiring musician without a major record deal and about to take his final degree exams; within three years, he had sold millions of albums and was dating a woman who earned millions of dollars for every film she appeared in. Obviously the money, cars, acclaim, adulation and success tempered his insecurities, but it is surely not as simple as one thinks. Kind of like the old bar-room boast of "I'd get in a ring with Mike Tyson for $10 million". Question is, would you ever get out again?

Chris makes no secret of the fact he thinks he has "the greatest job in the world". He has said that a different twist of fate might have seen him playing "Elton John covers in Marriott Hotels up and down the country", even offering up this disconcertingly accurate epitaph: "Enjoy the buffet, this is 'Rocket Man.'"

CHAPTER 17

Memories From My Father's Car

The year 2003 was a blur of gigs, award triumphs and an increasing frenzy surrounding Chris and Gwyneth's relationship. Despite wanting to keep the relationship relatively low-key and out of the spotlight, it was inevitable that the media weren't too accommodating. The engagement ring that Gwyneth had reportedly been sporting only whipped up the frenzy further. Speculation that the happy couple were about to get married was rife and magazines were even writing up 'details' of the forthcoming nuptials. In true Hollywood style – apparently – the legendary producer (and Gwyneth's godfather) Steven Spielberg would be walking the bride down the aisle and giving her away. Speaking on Virgin Radio – tongue firmly planted in his cheek – Chris said, "We are not getting married. Everything that is written about Steven and Chewbacca is a load of rubbish. Darth Vader is supposed to be giving her away. It is sad because it proves you can't believe anything you read in the papers." The intergalactic red herrings hid the actual practicalities of the situation, whereby a combination of Gwyneth mourning her father's sad passing and Coldplay's exhausting gig schedule made any pending wedding rather unlikely.

However, this didn't stop the rumours. Some magazines took the speculation one step further, suggesting that Gwyneth was going to be performing songs on the next Coldplay album, a notion that obviously worried the millions of fans, fearful of some Yoko Ono-esque collaboration and a growing rift within the ranks. Although no official comment was forthcoming, the tabloids in particular were keen to speculate how such a development might affect the internal politics of Coldplay. There was already an increasing instance of the band being called 'Chris Martin & Co' and although publicly the other three had never voiced concern about this singer-centric focus, it would not be the first time in rock history that such an imbalanced public interest had led to tension. While Chris was regularly in the spotlight with Gwyneth, the other three members of Coldplay remained resolutely private. Interviews with them are sparse and even then their answers are effusive, focused largely on the music and songs, with scant detail of their private lives. This was, in fact, a life that Chris hankered after; he was not a public personality by nature, but the band he fronted had become a huge global success and, by tradition, the lead singer received the majority of the attention. Add to that a relationship with a top Hollywood actress and it was a recipe for incessant high-profile intrusion. If Chris could have clicked his fingers and controlled how much press intrusion he tolerated, it's highly likely that, with the exception of the charity campaigns, there'd have been none.

That said, there were occasional rumours that the other three felt overshadowed – not by Chris himself, but by the public and media's perception of him, particularly when this wrongly implied he was the main or even sole creative force. However, they also acknowledged that such a profile could be a poisoned chalice: "It doesn't worry me that people think we don't do much," said Guy, "because I know we all work on everything together. I worry for the amount Chris is hassled by the paparazzi… Chris is single-minded, he's focused 24 hours a day. I've got a short attention span and want to switch off when I get home. Part of me wants to remain hidden – but that puts a lot of pressure on Chris."

As was so often the case, Chris had a typically light-hearted way to dismiss such rumours: "My entire life is spent trying to push [Guy Berryman] forward at photo shoots. He's our packaging ... he's a handsome bastard. None of us pretend that if he wasn't in the band we'd be as popular. He's responsible for all our calendar sales."

While the tabloids wrote yet more pieces on Chris and Gwyneth, the band were dominating many of 2003's award ceremonies. Most notably they scooped two coveted awards at the 45th Grammys, for 'Best Alternative Music Album' and 'Best Rock Vocal Performance By A Duo Or Group' for 'In My Place'. February's Brit Awards were equally successful, with 'Best British Group' and 'Best British Album' gongs heading Coldplay's way. MTV offered up 'Best Group Video' and 'Best Direction' for the classic video for 'The Scientist'. Even *NME* gave them both 'Best British Album' and 'Album Of The Year' trophies. In terms of critical acclaim, this represented about as broad a base as it was possible to get.

At the VMA ceremony at Radio City Music Hall, Chris dedicated that night's performance of 'The Scientist' to Johnny Cash, who had been due to attend the ceremony (to collect the award for 'Best Cinematography' on behalf of Jean-Yves Escoffier, who had photographed 'Hurt') but was unable to appear after he was taken ill and hospitalised. Before the show, Chris had been bemused when asked to crop the song's length, in order to fit into the rigidly tight TV schedules. On hearing that the ideal length would result in a quite dramatically truncated version, he simply said, "Why don't we just come out and bow without playing a note?" The playful mood was enhanced in rehearsals by Will repeatedly interrupting the mounting climactic drama of 'The Scientist' with a straight 4/4 punk rock beat, while Guy and Jon filled the endless waiting time by jamming numerous Rolling Stones songs. On the night the band were somewhat overshadowed by Madonna kissing Britney Spears and Christina Aguilera in an onstage 'lesbian romp' that sent a predictably salacious tabloid world into a whirlwind of seedy headlines. 'Madonna and Britney Do It One More Time' undoubtedly sells more newspapers than 'Chris and Guy change song timing to 4/4'!

Chris had made no secret of his adoration of Johnny Cash. The influence was obviously much deeper than a superficial nod of respect due to Cash's ill health. Chris's father had frequently played Cash's music in the family car when he was a child and the man's voice and work made an impact on him even at a young age: "He's my hero. His voice was bonkers… it sounded like this alien guy from America – which to me then was a million miles away – and here was this guy from the heart of it." The band had even begun work on a song for Cash, entitled 'Til Kingdom Come', going so far as to record some of the musical backing with the production legend Rick Rubin in Los Angeles. The track was virtually ready for Cash to come in and add his vocals; then, one day, Rubin arrived at the studio in LA and said, "Johnny's ill…" Johnny Cash never recovered from the diabetes-related complications that he had been battling, and passed away on September 12, 2003, before the track could be completed. (In 2006, Chris appeared with numerous other musicians in the posthumous Cash video for 'God's Gonna Cut You Down', alongside artists such as Iggy Pop, Kanye West, Justin Timberlake and Bono, to name but a few.)

Chris and the band were collaborating with other acts at this time too. Chris wrote a song called 'Gravity', which Coldplay had performed live back in 2002. Ultimately Chris decided to give the song to Embrace, the West Yorkshire rock outfit who had been hailed by many as the natural successors to Oasis. That band's lead singer, Danny McNamara, had first met Chris when Coldplay supported Embrace at The Blackpool Express Ballroom back in 2000 and they had been firm friends ever since. Explaining why he didn't record the track himself, Chris said he felt "it became clear… that the song might be better suited to Embrace. We've always loved Embrace and Danny is one of my best friends." The song was a big success for the band, and was their 'comeback' single (a number seven hit) ahead of the chart-topping 2004 album *Out Of Nothing* (Coldplay would later record their own version as a B-side to the single 'Talk', released late in 2005). Elsewhere, Chris penned the hit song 'See It In A Boy's Eyes' for Jamelia, written entirely from the perspective of a woman, a very accomplished and convincing piece of musical ghostwriting.

Later in 2003, the band themselves had their own cover version, recording The Pretenders' festive classic, '2000 Miles'. The song was available for a limited time as a download at coldplay.com, with benefits going to the Future Forests and Stop Handgun Violence charities. It was later recognised as 2003's most downloaded single, ahead of OutKast's 'Hey Ya!'. Statistically, this figure would soon be dwarfed as the phenomenon of downloads surged ahead and the physical single almost became obsolete within a few years; but for now, it was perhaps surprising that Coldplay – a band often wrongly criticised for having 'fairweather fans' who might only buy one CD or go to one concert a year – were carrying the download torch…

CHAPTER 18

New Beginnings

The band's continuing interest in Fair Trade may have annoyed the more cynical corners of the music press, but the reality was that the more Coldplay discovered about the commercial imbalance that existed in the trading world, the more incensed and motivated they became to help change that situation. It seems churlish to criticise people for using their power – whether it is through politics, music or fame – to effect change for good, but such is the poisoned chalice that a pop star holds.

In his defence, Chris is a highly educated champion of the cause; this was not a brief and cocooned dash in and back out of the African plains for a TV special, with cameras and PAs in attendance. For example, as the Coldplay juggernaut had trekked its way around South America, Jonny and Chris travelled to Puebla, a small village 90-minutes drive from Mexico City, where local maize farmers were struggling to compete with heavily subsidised American imports. On the same trip, Martin handed over a petition to Supachai Panitchpakdi, the World Trade Organisation director-general, containing three million signatures collected by Oxfam pressing for change in global trade. Although Panitchpakdi eventually got an autograph for his daughter, this was not before Chris had besieged him with insightful and difficult questions about subsidies and prohibitive tariffs, clearly informed by extensive research. One weapon that rock stars are equipped with when faced by lofty dignitaries and politicians is confidence – chatting in front of 50,000 fans makes sitting in one room with one person seem like a breeze. In addition, campaigning rock stars – or at least the good ones – take no notice of reputation or etiquette, as any person in power who has met Bob Geldof could confirm. Chris seemed to be cut from a similar cloth; although he was clearly not as fiery or daunting as the Boomtown Rats frontman, he was equally not averse to putting people on the spot. When he met Panitchpakdi he simply said, "You seem like a nice guy. Why is it so hard to get this problem sorted out?"

Chris's first trip to Haiti back in 2002 had convinced him that his privileged role as a rock star had to be used to benefit wider issues. His infamous wrist band, the Fair Trade flyers handed out at Coldplay gigs, extensive web links from their official site and countless other devices are repeatedly employed by Coldplay to further this – and other – causes. Chris is now firmly positioned in a long line of rock stars who have used their fame and sometimes their own money to champion numerous charities. The most obvious and famed case is clearly Band/Live Aid, for which Bob Geldof eventually earned the popular nickname 'Saint Bob' (his aim had been to raise £72,000 with the famous charity single; the whole project, including the Wembley gig, eventually made over £100 million). Another notable, and earlier, example would be George Harrison, whose 1971 Concert for Bangladesh is seen by many as a precursor to later rock-star charity events.

Coldplay were not averse to also assisting with more local campaigns too. When schoolgirl Sarah Sainsbury wrote to the band asking for their autographs to sell for her school's Breast Cancer Care charity, she was stunned to receive a package containing a highly valuable triple platinum disc. The disc – for *A Rush Of Blood To The Head* – was auctioned at a London fashion event for the huge sum of £4,000. In fact, the ceaseless charity gestures the band have made seem almost endless, but include: singing in a lucky competition winner's front room to 10 friends and family (in aid of a new resource centre for a primary school); auctioning a guitar lesson with Chris for £140,000 to support African AIDS-related charities; also auctioning a piano lesson, again with Chris, for thousands of pounds; providing free use of 'Fix You' to the United Way of London campaign to help society's vulnerable; sending a £3,000 piano to St David's Moreton-in-Marsh church school after it was devastated by floods in 2007, resulting in the music department having all its instruments wrecked; Chris performing on stage with Stevie Wonder to raise funds for fighting poverty in NYC; tweeting about the Chilean earthquake in 2010, which within minutes resulted in the Red Cross's website being swamped with offers of help and donations as it experienced a 400% increase in traffic; auctioning the chance to join Coldplay on stage at Madison Square Garden in 2003 – the winning bid was an astounding $500,000 for the privilege of singing 'In My Place'. On the rare occasions when their music has been used for a more commercial purpose, it has also been for a worthy cause. In 2005, for example, they donated the track 'Don't Panic' for free for the New Zealand blood donation service appeal to use. If the band had charged the going rate, it would have probably set the blood donation service back about half a million New Zealand dollars. The following year, the band again waived their usual aversion to 'commercials' by clearing free use of 'Fix You' by Cancer Research UK (this was particularly poignant for Gwyneth, whose father Bruce had succumbed to pneumonia and complications associated with cancer).

And it also wasn't just about raising money. In mid-2007, an Oxfam survey concluded that 84% of 18-24 year old British people know about that charity's campaigning work because of Coldplay. Surely all of this is a good thing?

As 2003 headed towards a close, the gossip-hungry tabloids and the superficial world of celebrity headlines actually had something concrete to report. First, Chris and Gwyneth confirmed that they were expecting a baby. The famously private couple were especially guarded about the pregnancy, but actually this wasn't just due to fear of media intrusion – Gwyneth admitted that she was also quite superstitious and, like many mothers, felt that discussing the sex of the unborn baby, the due dates and various other (private) details might somehow be a bad idea.

Then – suddenly – Chris and Gwyneth were married. No family or friends were present at the ceremony, only the happy couple and a judge in a Santa Barbara hotel. "I guess you can say we eloped. It was great because we got married without any fuss," Chris told *The Sun*.

Elsewhere, Chris likened himself to Hugh Grant's geeky, shy English fop in *Notting Hill*, who runs a bookshop and falls in love with a beautiful American film star (played by Julia Roberts). He then spends much of the movie avoiding the prying eyes of a fascinated world media pack. There are certainly similarities – the shyness, the slightly self-deprecating English humour, the awkwardness with his private life being made public – but it's hard to see a stuttering Hugh Grant holding 100,000 fans in the palm of his hand.

Nonetheless, the parallel was not entirely without merit. "I'd have eloped even if I wasn't famous and ran a shop," he said, as if to reinforce the comparison. Often harshly criticised for being 'boring', Chris and Gwyneth actually just live their life, generally in private, in the way they wish. They do lead what might be considered a fairly puritan life, with talk of macrodiets, a total abstinence from drugs, smoking and excessive alcoholic consumption – none of which fits the rock or movie star stereotype. Yet Chris has never claimed to be anything else, and Gwyneth was certainly never an actress renowned for Wildean antics before they met.

Over Christmas 2003, Chris and Gwyneth spent time in both New York and Los Angeles, getting ready for the impending arrival of their baby (although their luxury Belgravia flat remained their family home). It was noticeable that during this exciting time Chris – and to a certain extent Gwyneth – became understandably sensitised to the continued intrusions of the media, particularly the paparazzi. Chris had never been best buddies with the roving photographers, as this quote from earlier in the decade shows: "I'm no different to anyone else. Sometimes I react, but I don't go round punching photographers." On occasion, however, the tension had boiled over. During one visit to Australia, Chris was charged with malicious damage after allegedly damaging a photographer's car, although the charges were later dropped. Back in London in the spring of 2004, an allegation was made by a photographer that he had been kicked by Chris outside a restaurant in Knightsbridge. The Coldplay spokesman told BBC News Online that, "Naturally enough for a man whose wife is heavily pregnant with her first child, Chris' sole concern was to ensure that Gwyneth got into the cab safely and was not impeded or harassed in any way." Chris accepted a police caution for common assault.

Yet Chris was disarmingly honest when he acknowledged a degree of double standards about this aspect of his life. He openly admitted that while he was almost always incensed when fans asked him about some scurrilous tabloid story that had been made up about him and Gwyneth, by contrast he was himself no stranger to reading celebrity magazines. At least he admitted to feeling guilty and "cursing myself"!

The couple's unborn baby continued to make headlines, with rather invasive reports detailing exactly which strand of yoga classes they were attending, the type of birth they were planning (water birth) and even which hospital they were likely to attend. Gwyneth remained relatively quiet on the topic, although speaking on TV she did say that there was one downside to having a British-born child: "The only problem is he can never be President of the United States." No pressure then!

When she did speak in public about the impending arrival, Gwyneth made no secret of her immense admiration for her movie star mother, Blythe Danner, who had put her own ascending career on hold to bring up Gwyneth and her brother Jake. "My mother turned down every fantastic movie there was," Paltrow told *W Magazine*. "She turned down these amazing things that would have made her a huge movie star." And she took a sideswipe at high-profile actresses who choose to continue their full careers after giving birth, saying they must "literally never see" their children.

Then, in the middle of May, Gwyneth went into labour and gave birth to a baby girl, weighing in at a healthy 9lbs and 11 ounces. In typically poetic fashion, Chris said, "We are 900 miles over the moon, and we'd like to thank everyone at the hospital who have looked after us amazingly."

Their first-born was given the name Apple Blythe Alison. Reportedly, the name Apple might have been inspired by Marty Diamond's, Coldplay's North American booking agent, little girl (although he claimed it was a coincidence); similarly, Gwyneth's *Shallow Hal* director Peter Farrelly also has a daughter with the same Christian name; her middle names, Blythe and Alison, were taken from her grandmothers. With justification, Chris was in no mood to debate the rights and wrongs of unusual child names: "What I call my baby is none of anyone's business," he told *Details* magazine. "When we first told everyone we were Coldplay, they addressed us like we just said we bought a house on Mars. I think it's a cool name, so why does it matter?"

Bob Geldof's daughter Peaches warned that she had suffered years of taunts at school over her unusual name, including the possibly apocryphal line, "Oi, Peaches, are your parents bananas?" In their defence, Apple was positively conservative compared to a long list of unusual rock star baby names, not least Frank Zappa's daughter Moon-Unit and Bowie's son Zowie. More recently, My Chemical Romance's Gerard Way called his daughter Bandit.

Comedian and close friend Simon Pegg was later asked to be Apple's godfather. Other reports 'detailed' phone calls congratulating the couple coming from the superstar likes of Madonna, Stella McCartney and Sadie Frost, which if true confirmed the level of hyper-celebrity that the Coldplay singer now mixed in. Perhaps all of these glittering celebs were overshadowed by the news that a type of the fruit was going to be named in the baby's honour. Chief executive of English Apples & Pears Ltd, Adrian Barlow, said he was delighted that they had named their baby daughter "after such a popular fruit" and went on to reveal that "We decided to name our next variety 'The Paltrow' in honour of the birth."

Only days after the birth of baby Apple, Coldplay's official website featured a video by a band called The Nappies. The footage featured a familiar-looking four-piece wearing glam-rock wigs, tight clothes and looking generally like a shambolic version of Spinal Tap. Among the gems they offered was a rap from the 'lead singer' of The Nappies, who performed to his wife and baby, offering the emotional promise that he would always be there for them and went on to reference "poo" and "sick" as well as the maternally inflated size of Gwyneth's breasts. (Gwyneth would later rap the song herself during an exclusive appearance on *The Oprah Winfrey Show*.)

In another nod to the feverish interest surrounding their new arrival, Chris arranged for baby Apple to 'meet' the world's press, who were camped outside their Belgravia home. It gave the media their "one and only chance to photograph them for a very long time". Gwyneth walked a black pram outside for around five minutes and chatted happily with the 20 or so photographers and journalists in attendance, telling them she was very happy and that the baby was doing really well. Later, the family moved to a much bigger house in a leafy north London suburb populated by many film and rock stars, such as Jude Law and Gwen Stefani, when they bought *Titanic* star Kate Winslet's house, which offered a much higher level of privacy. Reports coincided with this that Paltrow had put her four-storey townhouse in Manhattan's trendy Greenwich Village up for sale in excess of £4 million.

Understandably, baby Apple had made the couple even more sensitive to the perils of celebrity life and Gwyneth made it clear that she would press charges if she felt a line had been crossed. Speaking to *The Telegraph*, she said, "In London, they chase you in cars, and I will start pressing charges because they're endangering me by the way they drive. It's really scary. It's just unacceptable, especially when there's the life of a small baby in your hands." She also stated that she had started making notes on the photographers whom she felt were too frequently being invasive. "It's really frustrating. I wish people would just let us get on with it once in a while and let us have a normal day together."

Gwyneth seemed so blissfully happy with motherhood and Apple that many industry observers suggested she might never act again; however, speaking to the press, she qualified premature reports that she had in fact retired: "I'm going to take a break for a little while. Reports of my retirement are exaggerated. But when you have a baby, it reorganises your priorities. I want to go back to work, but right now I just want to be with Apple. I feel great and the best thing about being a mum is her. She is just the most gorgeous, sweet, lovely girl in the world." When Gwyneth eventually returned to acting, it was only to sing one song in the opening scene of *What Is This Thing Called Love?*, where she played the role of Peggy Lee and was reportedly paid a whopping £2 million for that single song.

Fatherhood had certainly also impacted hugely on Chris. "Everything's great," he enthused to www.online.ie. "I've just been writing lyrics and doing baby things. It's great man, it's the best thing that's ever happened. If someone told me my life at the moment would be changing nappies and writing lyrics I would've taken it, y'know? It's my dream come true."

CHAPTER 19

Off The Radar

"I can't stand the way the guy sells millions of albums, plays stadiums, marries a Hollywood star and complains about the paparazzi. That comes with the territory. It's a horrible name, Coldplay. It doesn't conjure up any positive thoughts. He looks like he's on the verge of a panic attack."

Ian Brown

By stark contrast, while 2004 is a year that Chris and Gwyneth will never forget on a personal level, professionally it was Coldplay's quietest period to date. However, this is somewhat misleading, since the band was busy working on material for the next album. Yet above the parapet, it was a time when they made virtually no public appearances, with scant gigs and, according to *NME*, only one interview. They began to be referred to as 'reclusive', which was not an altogether negative development. Chris had been concerned that the band's recent seeming omnipotence and commercial dominance would result in people getting bored of them through overexposure. The year 2004 provided a chance to reflect, calm down and look back at all they had achieved. After all, only a few years ago Coldplay were unsigned. Chris told *The Sun* that, "I want time off because I've had a mad year. I think people need a rest from Coldplay. There's a real pressure on us now, too. We've become obsessed with trying to deliver something amazing. I hope people aren't sick of us ... I'm always worried it could end tomorrow. There's no guarantee people are not going to get fed up with us ..."

Mark E. Smith, enigmatic frontman of The Fall, had already had enough, and after recounting a story about the band allegedly being mistaken for stockbrokers in New York, he criticised Coldplay for being overly interested in money and business. Never one to make dull statements however, Chris had an interesting theory about self-belief and self-awareness: "I reckon everybody questions whether they're useful to the world or not. Some people think they're doing marvellous things. Hitler thought he was doing great things for the world, and yet we'd all say, 'No, no, no, he was doing terrible things.' Some people would say that Coldplay is a great thing for music and the world. Other people would regard us as the devil incarnate, so of course it's always a conflict."

Although this quiet time was a direct consequence of hectic private lives and exhausting recording schedules, the end result was that, for a time at least, Coldplay dropped off the radar.

The year began very publicly, however, with another Grammy. At that year's Grammys, they won 'Record Of The Year' for 'Clocks' but were humbled when their heart-breaking vignette for 'The Scientist' was beaten to the trophy for 'Best Short Form Video' by the late Johnny Cash's 'Hurt'. Chris dedicated their own award to Johnny Cash and then expressed his support – like most of the entire musical and creative world – for the leading Democratic presidential hopeful John Kerry by saying he will "hopefully will be your president one day". Despite being perfectly entitled to voice an opinion, he faced an immediate and fairly virile backlash from fans and observers criticising his decision to back a candidate for elections in a country where he did not reside. This was a time of increased sensitivity in TV circles, coming only a week after Janet Jackson's infamous 'wardrobe malfunction' during a Superbowl performance during which her breast had been exposed to millions of American families during a duet with Justin Timberlake. But for Brits already used to Chris airing his views – as he'd previously made statements during awards ceremonies about the Iraq war and also attacked President Bush during the Brit Awards – this seemed like a storm in a tea cup.

In autumn 2003, attention had turned to thoughts of the next album and there were already multiple ideas and demos in existence before the Christmas break. Chris and Jon had committed quite a few ideas to tape during a trip to Chicago, for example. At the end of January, Coldplay reconvened at a London studio to begin formal work on the next record. Again working with Ken Nelson, the four began work in Liverpool's Parr Street studio before moving on to Air Studios in London. By mid 2004, Coldplay were sufficiently 'reclusive' in the eyes of the media that any interviews given were described as 'rare' or 'elusive'. Generally, Chris would only surface to further the Fair Trade cause, but inevitably snippets emerged about the development of the new record. In an odd moment of Liam Gallagher-esque bravado, he said that they were "trying to make the best thing that anyone has ever heard. My philosophy at the moment in life is why not try and be Einstein, even if you're never going to make it."

Even when he did surface in public, it was generally with as little fuss as possible – for example, at the premiere of the zombie-Brit-flick *Shaun Of The Dead*, he attended with Will and Guy but said nothing to the press as he sprinted in the entrance and later left by a back door. Chris had a cameo in the film wandering around a dark street as a zombie. For the movie's soundtrack, Chris paired up with Irish power-pop act Ash for a cover of Buzzcocks' 'Everybody's Happy Nowadays' (later included as a B-side on Ash's 'Orpheus' single). Later, in 2010, when Ash released their single 'Binary', the spoof horror mini-movie they'd filmed many years previously – with Chris and Jonny making a small cameo – was used in the accompanying video.

As the year progressed, a few rare nuggets of information slipped out about some of the intriguing directions and influences on the new album, with Chris talking of listening to Kraftwerk and Jay-Z as well as his new daughter (not surprisingly) being a lyrical and thematic inspiration. After those initial Chicago demos, work in London and then New York with Ken Nelson progressed in private and without apparent incident. The July sessions in the Big Apple were seen as the effective start of the album recordings proper. The process was organic but not initially fluid. Beginning with banks of technology, the band – by their own admission – inadvertently distanced themselves from the live energy of a four-piece group playing together. As they skitted from studio to studio, the momentum wasn't as strong as everyone hoped until they realised that they needed to get back to a more intimate 'band' vibe. There was even talk of them ditching many of the near-completed recordings and starting from scratch, such was their drive for perfection. "We all went to a bar in Liverpool," Chris told *Rolling Stone*, "and said, 'We need to sort this out, because it's not right.' It sounded like four people playing different things and then chucking it into a computer to edit it and fix it."

In a great slice of pop irony, when explaining the reasoning behind scrapping so many of the songs during the increasingly tempestuous recording process, Chris revealed the most unlikely inspiration for having the bravery to start again – their fiercest critics, Mancunians Oasis. While watching a documentary about the making of the Gallagher brothers' classic *Definitely Maybe*, Chris realised that the Mancs had, part way through the recording sessions, stripped back to being just a live rock 'n' roll band.

Suitably refocused, Coldplay chose to disappear into a dark rehearsal room in north London – just the four of them, no producers or engineers or record label people – and work through ideas. They were a band again, just like they had been only a few years ago when still an unsigned act. It worked. Ken Nelson was soon brought in again to lend his expert ear and suddenly the creative momentum was back on track. Eventually, the 30-plus tracks were narrowed down to 15, and it was from this final cut that the album's dozen songs were chosen.

The rest of 2004 was filled with various sporadic announcements, fleeting media appearances and internet rumours. They were due to make a 'rare' appearance at a one-off benefit gig for Californian public radio station 89.9 FM KCRW in November, at the 6,000 capacity Universal Amphitheatre in Los Angeles. KCRW was the first radio station in America to play Coldplay in 2000, with the band making their US live radio début in December that year. However, due to reported "scheduling and logistical conflicts", the gig had to be rescheduled.

The band's former 'bed-wetting' 'knobhead' lead singer had risen to lofty new heights since those early disparaging comments, with *Esquire* magazine placing him in their list of 'Best Dressed Men', alongside hip-hop star André 3000 at the top (as well as Prince Charles). Chris was praised – apparently it's a compliment – for knowing "how to pull off today's hot high-low look, mixing a T-shirt and jeans with a suit jacket".

Just in case he was getting to believe his own hype though, old foe Alan McGee had another barbed riposte for Chris. When asked if he regretted his name being associated with his Mercury Music Prize outburst against the soft rockers, he said he did, only to qualify this admission by saying, "I really regret making that Coldplay comment. It made Coldplay a lot more interesting than they actually are." Towards the end of 2004, however, the enigmatic label legend seemed to draw a line under the whole 'feud' when he said, "It was an off-the-cuff, bizarre Northern remark really. I don't get off on their music, but eight million people do, so good luck to them."

One brief but typically successful release during this period of studio activity came when Fierce Panda issued 'Brothers & Sisters' as a download on their new service via The Orchard. Coldplay's early effort became iTunes' second most downloaded record and hung around the Top 10 for over a month. In September 2004, Chris made an unexpected live appearance that was – again – tied to a charitable cause, when he performed with REM at Oxfam's London Hammersmith Apollo show. Halfway through REM's 'Man On The Moon', Chris sprang on stage much to the surprise of the capacity audience, where he then sang a verse and chorus before waving at the crowd and retreating to watch the rest of the show from the side of the stage.

Media interviews were almost nonexistent during this time. *NME* billed its lengthy chat with Chris during 2004 as the band's 'only magazine interview this year' no less. In the piece, Chris offered some enticing glimpses behind the scenes of their secretive new album sessions. Telling *NME* that he was particularly inspired by Michael Stipe and 'Losing My Religion', he acknowledged the band were feeling an "immense" amount of pressure to follow up *A Rush Of Blood To The Head*, which was now widely seen by most critics as a classic second album. "We're working all the time because it's so important. We can't fuck it up." And in an effort to minimise the criticism of his "reinvent the wheel" comment after their brilliant V 2003 show, he offered the defence that it was "just post-gig excitement! We're just trying to redesign it, not reinvent it. We're one receded inch away [from finishing]. When my hair's gone back another inch, I know we'll have finished our album."

Ensconced in their studio, beavering away on the album, Coldplay made no secret of the fact that they would prefer not to be disturbed. However, some approaches just can't be rebuffed and so it was when Sir Bob Geldof contacted them to appear on a new version of the classic Band Aid single, 'Do They Know It's Christmas?', under the banner of Band Aid 20. The project's title was a nod to the legendary record's 20th anniversary and the idea was designed to benefit Sudan's troubled Darfur region. Geldof was again joined at the helm by Ultravox's Midge Ure, but this time they were eager not to revisit the famous studio scenes of two decades' previous, which had seen the likes of Duran Duran, Status Quo and Phil Collins perform on the multi-million-selling single 'Do They Know It's Christmas?'

For this fresh version they wanted a new generation to be heavily involved, and so the rumour mills went into full swing about who would appear. Chris later told the media that he had initially thought the project might be a bad idea – having to live up to its illustrious predecessor – but after having watched footage of the appalling humanitarian disaster in the Darfur region of Sudan, he couldn't help fast enough.

On November 14, 2004 the élite of British rock and pop began working on the track at Air Studios, overseen by the commanding and iconic figure of Geldof and his long-term ally Midge Ure. Coldplay were joined by, among others, Danny Goffey (Supergrass), Thom Yorke and Jonny Greenwood of Radiohead, Fran Healy from Travis, Justin Hawkins of The Darkness and even Sir Paul McCartney on bass (one of only three artists, along with Bono and George Michael, to be retained from the original line-up). Chris sang the opening line of the track, originally performed 20 years' earlier by Paul Young.

Although it was impossible to fully replicate the phenomenon of the 1984 song, the new version did capture some of the same national spirit that made the first single such a colossal success. Major retailers, such as Woolworths and Virgin, vowed to hand over all proceeds, while even the government got in on the act, offering to waive VAT. The single became the UK's biggest-selling record of 2004, as well as the Christmas number one. A documentary entitled *Band Aid 20: Justice, Not Charity* showed behind-the-scenes footage of the new recording and further helped both sales and the project's profile.

When the track's video was ready for screening, the major broadcasters displayed an unprecedented show of support by changing their standard programming in order to premiere the video simultaneously. Consequently, a third of the population stopped to watch the promo clip on a range of channels (with an introduction by Madonna). The video included footage of Birhan Woldu, an Ethiopian survivor from the original 1984 famine.

With such colossal coverage and national support, it was no surprise that over 72,000 copies were sold on the first day alone, across chains of stores that opened early for the event. At the end of the week, in excess of 200,000 copies had been bought, more than the rest of the Top 30 combined. Bizarrely, the altered lyrics were criticised in some quarters for being 'patronising', which seemed churlish to say the least, and Chris was happy to dismiss these harsh comments as inappropriate. "It's not about the song or about the words, it is about the images you sometimes see in the videos."

Chris was also seen furthering the profile of other global poverty issues on TV at this time. In late 2004, speaking on a Jonathan Dimbleby special for ITV1, Chris spoke forthrightly about his aims: "It's really achievable, it's not a mystical thing ... it literally takes like 10 men ... to just sit round a table and say, 'Yeah why don't we change this law?', or 'Why don't we lower the tariff barrier on imports from Ghana?' or 'Why don't we stop sending so much surplus rice to Mexico?' It's very easy to do. That's why I'm excited because I feel like if people like me make the right albums and sell enough records ... [we] can [get to] talk to the right people."

He went on to explain that the arrival of Apple – far from making him insular – had energised him to redouble his efforts in tackling the issues for which he'd become a regular champion. "I'm like anybody else, you can either ignore it and just pretend it doesn't exist or, in my case, you can feel like you've been given so much that ... you have to take an interest in it. I've got a baby and I think if the world keeps going the way it is, it's going to be bad for everybody, not just for poor people, because it can't keep going the way it is, you know, trade the way it is, or AIDs the way it is. So I don't want to see the apocalypse."

Chris also took time to revisit some of the poorest regions of the world, where unfair trading conditions were still having a devastating effect on lives. He admitted that having been deep in recording studios for most of 2004, and with his own family life also being so busy, that these problems had – to use his own words – "started to become a bit hollow, because I started to forget what I was really talking about. It took 20 minutes of driving in a truck through farm land in Ghana to remind me why I'm doing it."

On this trip, however, there was a terrifying incident when his plane nearly crashed in Africa. As it approached Tamale Airport in Ghana, it was hit by an intense dust storm. Almost instantly, the pilot of the small aircraft could not see the landing strip, despite being at 200 metres altitude. Effectively flying blind, he struggled with both the lack of visibility and the raging wind. "The plane dropped off violently to the right, then way off to the left," Chris told Contactmusic.com. "It was lurching all over. It was so terrifying, my mind was racing and I thought, 'My daughter will have to get a stepdad.' I thought, 'I've written a will. The band haven't finished the album, but they know how I want to finish certain songs…'"

Somehow the pilot managed to land and Chris said this near-death experience futher reminded him of the precious nature of life: "It fired me up for the trip. I thought, 'I'm going to learn as much as I can and meet as many people as possible." Later, Chris hosted a half-hour MTV special about his trip, called *Chris Martin: Two Fingers To Poverty*.

CHAPTER 20

Alien Digital Rabbits Etc

While the music world had not expected the new Coldplay album to be released in 2004, when news began filtering out that the original spring 2005 release date was also going to be delayed it was greeted with some surprise. Immediately people whispered about internal tensions and the possibility of a split. Quotes from Chris inadvertently fuelled this speculation: "I still spend at least 60 per cent of my time thinking, 'I can't write songs,'" he later explained on XFM, recalling earlier career confidence worries. "I don't see myself as brilliantly talented, but lucky to have met the right combination of people who fit together like a jigsaw so you can't see our individual shortcomings."

An official newsletter was issued explaining that the delay was down to the band wanting to be totally ready to head back out on the road again, after such a lengthy time away from touring. Will was quoted as saying, "The prospect of touring again was so daunting that we felt we should take our time, and also we wanted to make sure that it [the album] was the best it could possibly be."

EMI perceived the new Coldplay album as its biggest global release of the year. For the record company, the news of a delay was, in fact, catastrophic. With the Coldplay record slipping into the next fiscal year (as did the new release by Damon Albarn's alter-ego animated über-band, Gorillaz), EMI were duty bound to issue a reduced profit forecast for the coming financial year end. And as EMI's earnings had dropped for three straight years in a row, the news was not received well by the City, with shares in the record label plummeting by an astonishing 18%.

Even the financial press chipped in, with some industry experts claiming that the resulting fall in EMI share prices and the subsequent delayed income stream could have potentially cost the label in the region of £320 million.

Initially the band gave themselves no new deadline; the March 2005 release date came and went and then eventually news broke that the album would be released in the early summer of 2005. Will explained that the lack of a deadline actually made the band less productive – echoing the age-old music biz saying, "If you have two years to record an album, you will take two years; if you have two weeks, you will record it in two weeks." Nonetheless, the delay proved far more productive for the band than it did for their beleaguered record label. In the last-minute extended sessions, some of the new record's finest tracks were created, because as Will says, "The best stuff comes when we start to panic."

Obviously aware of the conversations about EMI's share value, Chris remained unmoved by such monetary concerns and reinforced the notion that the record was much richer for the delay: "The one benefit of time is that we've had a chance to wait for proper songs to land. The last song that's on the album came out of a conversation I was having at home after we thought we'd finished. I explained that we were still missing that one song. I got really angry and aggressive and this song just came out in five minutes, and a week later it's all done."

Notably, the band themselves also reportedly missed out on substantial financial bonuses by delaying the release. Although Chris did not confirm this directly, he told XFM: "Deadlines be damned. It was all to do with fiscal years and shareholders anyway. Once we forgot about the money, we were free to push ourselves to the very limits and make the best album possible." No doubt EMI shareholders felt a chill down the spine when the ever-confusing Chris Martin announced this could still be the band's last ever album.

During the delay, Will and Chris did take time out to perform a very intimate gig to members of Parlophone at London's Whitfield

Street Studios (also playing that night were labelmates Idlewild, The Departure and Athlete, plus audio previews of new Gorillaz tracks). Although only playing two songs, the acoustic performance was an exciting teaser of what was to come. One song was introduced as 'A Message', while the second, untitled track was simply called "our Johnny Cash song". Chris also said not to judge the album by this latter tune, because "track 12 is very obscure [and] it's the only one we can do at the moment".

Finally, Coldplay fans (and EMI executives) the world over had a release date: June 6, 2005. The first single was to be a track called 'Speed Of Sound', due for release a couple of weeks earlier on May 23. Early fears that the band would veer wildly off the beaten Coldplay track with a drastic change of direction were quickly allayed when Jonny was quoted as saying, "We wanted to try new things out, to move our sound along, but the focus remains on the songs, and Chris's voice is sounding amazing. Everyone is playing at the top of their game."

Two months before the album was due to hit the shelves, the band made a stunning return to the live arena with a low-key gig at the famous Troubadour venue in Los Angeles, ahead of the delayed benefit show for KCRW Radio. The 400 capacity venue was obviously rammed. Matters weren't helped by Chris suffering from a nasty throat infection, but the band soldiered on regardless.

Another high-profile 'secret' show was for MTV, where among those in attendance was Oasis's Noel Gallagher. His brother, Liam, decided against going; when asked by a reporter if he had attended, he rolled up his shirt sleeves and said, "Do you see razor-blade marks? That's what you'd see if I'd been to see them."

During this pre-release period, *NME* interviewed Chris and he seemed on top form, ever self-deprecating and flitting between bombastic ambition and shatteringly fragile self-confidence. "We've still got so much work to do. I need a day off and we haven't even started. We're still trying to finish the album. There's always things to be done." Despite the gigs being welcomed feverishly and the previously critical media showing many signs of being predisposed to supporting the new album, Chris quickly seemed to convince himself that the band were facing an uphill battle. "Being in Coldplay and coming back now is very different to what it was three years ago. There's a lot more eyes on us so you don't feel like you have any time to sort things out properly. I know there are some good songs on there ... I remember feeling like this on the last record, terrified."

Far from reinventing the wheel as he had so famously proclaimed before the album was recorded, Chris was happy to admit that the band had ultimately remained relatively close to the sounds and writing style they were famed for. Rather than burying their 'soft rock' style, as had been suggested back in 2003, they had in fact honed a sound that they were already global pioneers of: "I realised that you can only really reinvent your own wheel and the main thing to me was that our wheel was our songs. We've written a bunch of songs now that are pushing us further than we've ever been before and so in terms of our point of view we have done it. In terms of the wider world, we haven't worked out how to make a new instrument or a new time signature but it's not all about bleeps and squeaks."

Then finally it was time for something concrete: the new single, 'Speed Of Sound', released at the end of May 2005. Opening with a trademark piano riff, the song has all the facets of a classic Coldplay song: seductive drums, ethereal synth-backing, fragile falsetto vocals, scorching guitar. It's a package that they create better than anyone else and here, on this new single, it was done with considerable aplomb. The huge and upbeat chorus is synth-driven and destined to fill stadiums across the world. Guy admitted that they had been listening to Kate Bush's seminal 'Running Up That Hill' and had tried to mimic the track's distinctive drums, only for the sessions to splinter off into this exciting new composition.

EMI must have breathed a huge sigh of relief, as early signs suggested it was on course to become the fastest and biggest download single of all time. And not just in Britain either – by midweek, the song was at number one in the download charts of every international market. In addition, 'Speed Of Sound' was also one of the most requested songs on American radio stations. And yet, despite all the hype, when the chart was announced on the Sunday night, the self-acclaimed 'Annoying Thing', Crazy Frog, beat 'Speed Of Sound' to the top spot with its reworking of 'Axel F' – the theme to Eddie Murphy's hit movie *Beverly Hills Cop*. Reports had the Frog – who had started life as a ringtone advert cartoon – outselling

Coldplay by four to one in some stores (shades of Ultravox's 'Vienna' being kept off the top spot by Joe Dolce's 'Shaddap You Face'). However, the band were buoyed by the fact that the single stayed in the Top 75 for over four months. And when the physical CD purchases were combined with the colossal download sales, 'Speed Of Sound' became Coldplay's most successful single to date. Then the news broke from across the pond: Coldplay had become the first British band since The Beatles to have a new entry in the *Billboard* Top 10 singles chart, when the new track went in at number eight on its first week of release. The predecessor was The Beatles' 'Hey Jude' in 1968. Many observers noted that the band's success in the States was arguably linked to their exposure in successful TV series; there was the use of 'Trouble' during the finale of *Without A Trace*, 'Fix You' during a dramatic heart attack scene in *The OC*, and 'Clocks' on *ER*. This is undoubtedly true, but it shouldn't dilute the impact of the extensive US touring undertaken by the band for years beforehand.

Despite the single's commercial success, reviews were decidedly mixed, with more than one critic pointing out the similarity to 'Clocks'. Nonetheless, the track went on to receive two Grammy nominations, for 'Best Rock Song' and 'Best Rock Performance By A Duo Or Group With Vocals' at the 2006 Grammy Awards. A Brit for 'Best British Single' and an MTV award for 'Best Song', as well as Ivor Novello nominations for 'Most Performed Work' and 'International Hit of the Year', also followed. It was an impressive return. Coldplay were back. The question now was, would the album live up to expectations?

In a new-found digital world, where the record business was still reeling from the seismic impact of the download phenomenon, the security surrounding the new Coldplay album was immense. Rather than mail out physical CDs to eminent reviewers, journalists were asked to attend a room at EMI where they were played the album via an iPod placed inside a glass case, surrounded by security guards. It wasn't just the security around the album that was innovative: there were also plans to run a Bluetooth campaign (said to be a world first), whereby six large screens in London stations would transmit Bluetooth clips of album trailers, screen savers and photography, as well as selected musical extracts, direct to commuters' mobiles. This was christened 'bluecasting'.

The intriguing new album title and artwork was the subject of endless internet speculation about the exact meaning of the cryptic design. Some suggested it was alien code, or a digitised rabbit; others said the colour coding was related to the band's Chinese horoscopes; or maybe it was a peculiar bar code; still others said that if the artwork was minimised and viewed at just the right angle, a new picture would be produced, similar to the famous painting by Hans Holbein called 'The Ambassadors'; or was it all perhaps an obtuse reference to the male and female chromosomes?

All of this was, obviously, rubbish. There was indeed some significance to the new artwork, but it wasn't alien digital rabbits. Numerous websites, such as www.sleevage.com, analysed the artwork and successfully cracked the 'code'. The blocks on the cover were actually arranged in a code that was originally developed in 1874 by a scientist called Émile Baudot, whose idea was to use the system for transmitting telegraph messages. The blocks are visual representations of ones and zeros in a five-digit sequence that corresponds with parts of the alphabet and other topographic symbols. A precursor to Morse code, some science historians regard this system as the very first incarnation of digital communication. Technically speaking, it is actually called ITA2, a five-bit alphanumeric encoding used by telegraphs.

Given that a coloured block is a one and a blank block is a zero, the Coldplay artwork reads (down) as 10111… which is the letter X. The right-hand column reads as 10101, namely Y. You can probably guess what the middle column represents… '&'? Wrong, there was no ampersand in Baudot's original code, so the digit '9' is used instead.

Inside the sleeve artwork, the entire Baudot alphabet is included. The sleeve packaging was designed by artists Mark Tappin and Simon Gofton (known professionally as Tappin Gofton). The final page of the booklet even contains the slogan 'Make Trade Fair' using this coding. That would be great if the delegates or politicians being lobbied are fluent in ITA2 coding. Strangely, in south-east Asia and Holland, the coding on the album's front cover was replaced with standard photos of the whole band.

Of course, this just tells us what the colour-coding meant; it doesn't tell us *why* the album was called *X&Y*. Eventually Chris revealed all: "X and

Y is the mathematical formula used when you don't know the answer. But it's also like black and white, or hope and despair, or optimism and pessimism. Everywhere you look there's a tension of opposites."

The pessimistic side went into overdrive three months before the record's release when shock rumours of an internet leak of the *entire* new album began to spread around the web like a bushfire. For every Coldplay fan that was outraged, there were a thousand music fans who were no doubt rummaging wildly around trying to locate the mp3 files. By now, such leaks had become a common feature of the record release process. Nevertheless, Coldplay were appalled, and their lawyers and tech teams pounced on the rumours; fortunately, it quickly became apparent that there was in fact no such leak and a collective sigh of relief was breathed all round. One site, which appeared to have titles of songs by the band from the new album, actually just had mp3 files that, when downloaded, played only static noise.

However, there was one last-minute hiccup. Another story broke of a leak on the internet just a week before the album's release and this time it was not a hoax. It coincided with the album having been sent out to radio stations, although on this occasion EMI was much more philosophical. A spokesman stated that it was, "Kinda OK... I'm not saying we condone it but I'm not saying it's a disaster". This represented a seismic shift in the label's attitude; when the 'hoax' leak occured some months before, the entire label had been devastated and there was serious commercial panic. However, in just those few short months the landscape had changed enormously and many bands and labels were beginning to see that leaks were sometimes advantageous – in terms of PR – provided the consumer still went out and bought a legitimate copy. It also helped that the leak was only a week before the official launch, and in the case of Japan it came the day before the CD hit stores.

CHAPTER 21

X&Y

When Coldplay first broke through, the derisory comments about being 'Radiohead-lite' were at times suffocating. However, while Thom Yorke's band of experimentalists veered off into increasingly abstract territory with albums like *Kid A* and *Amnesiac*, the audience that had fallen for *OK Computer* (in itself not exactly a straightforward record) started to look for more straightforward musical landscapes. While Radiohead's sales remained high and their live shows became increasingly enormous, for every fan who adored the dark and obtuse canvas of *Kid A,*there were many more who found the work just too difficult.

When Coldplay arrived, this was definitely a factor in their early success – although they have joked themselves about mimicking Radiohead, the doors opened by the Oxford outfit proved invaluable to those that followed. However, it wasn't just Coldplay; others invited themselves to the party too. Athlete, Keane and Snow Patrol are the most obvious examples. While Coldplay were working on – and then delaying – their third album, these acts all threatened to steal their crown as the nation's favourite 'soft rock' act. Not that they would have seen it like that themselves, of course. But nonetheless, when *X&Y* was finally released, they had some formidable rivals. The question was: could the new album reinstate the band at the top of the tree?

X&Y opens with what sounds like a sister record to 'Politik'. An ambient synth-drenched and wistful electronica backing leads in to a typically melancholic Chris vocal, only for it to erupt after less than a minute into a full-on scorching guitar-driven explosion. The listener is immediately thrown into a record of vast arena rock. When the song progresses to a bass-led mid-section, the shades of lithe bass playing by U2's Adam Clayton and the effects pedal genius of The Edge are all too apparent. But that is not really a criticism, since Coldplay add lashings of their own stylings and create a brilliant album opener.

'What If' – *sans* question mark – strips the record right back to what we expect from Coldplay. However, when the band are 'predictable' they always do it *so well*. Even when you know that the piano and fragile vocal will undoubtedly lead to a slight build in momentum, a few lush strings and, ultimately, a heartfelt song, they still nail it. It sounds like a simple formula – yet is anything but. It's easy to analyse, but nearly impossible to mimic. Fans speculated over whether the wistful lyrics were an ode to Gwyneth or perhaps to the fanbase. Whichever was correct, Chris's glass-like self-confidence was wafer thin here. Next up is the Prince-like 'White Shadows', set against a stunningly simple tub-thumping drum line, achingly basic vocal textures and very precise, controlled yet brutally simplistic riffing from Jonny. This time the song effortlessly builds towards a momentous climax, with a neat chorus and massive lyrical hook that drives the song towards its conclusion. Even then, Chris is unafraid to end with exposed vocals and simple synth chords, which reinforces that odd conundrum in terms of his self-confidence – while he may battle constantly with his confidence, on record he is almost fearless about exposing his voice and inner emotions.

Then it's on to an obvious album highlight: 'Fix You'. It is the album's strongest ballad – no mean feat – and had a fantastic impact every time it was played live. Opening with a simple church organ chord progression, this is one of Chris's finest vocal moments. Even as his voice wavers in the opening verse, the warbles are endearing. This is no technically perfect virtuoso performance by a diva more concerned with vocal acrobatics; this is a lyric sung with genuine sincerity. One can only speculate about his thoughts as he sang the universally brilliant lines (and boy did people speculate!). However, Chris wisely always keeps his counsel with regard to specific lyric meanings. When the chorus leads to the closing titular lyric, it is breathtaking. Yet somehow the rest of the band manage to ramp it up still further, with Jonny's stabbing guitar riff eventually tumbling into a heavy-handed and brutally emotional drum line, producing a heart-rending climax to the song. The band's choir-like vocals push the song to its ending and the simple device of closing with the 'fix you' lyric is modest genius.

The U2 comparisons are perhaps a little too stark on future third single, 'Talk', although there are clear shades of Kraftwerk too; prior to release, Coldplay had chatted openly about the revered electronic pioneers Kraftwerk – conversations that must have given EMI and Coldplay's more conservative fans apoplexy – but fortunately their influence on the album was not full-on. Here, a hook from the German band's 1981 track 'Computer Love' was authorised by Kraftwerk for inclusion. To criticise is harsh, to a degree, as the song is creative, has appealing flavours of Germanic rock and even slices of folk that mingle very well. Jonny is the song's star, using ultra-melodic jangles, massive chord smashes and finely honed detail to stunning effect. Yet another stadium classic.

The title track is perhaps – oddly – the album's weakest moment. Chris's vocals open against the expected synth backdrop, but by the time the psychedelic chorus crashes in, the melodic interest is waning and the song sounds rather tired. There are occasional snippets of Pink Floyd influence that are perhaps not expected on a Coldplay album. However, the near-sitar guitar parts and Sixties vocalisation seem to jar.

The lead single, 'Speed Of Sound', is up next, neatly sitting in the middle of the album, starting off 'the so-called (second) Y side'. Of all the tracks here, it is probably the most predictable, although this is not necessarily a criticism. The listener could have been forgiven for thinking they had put the début album on when the next track, 'A Message', strikes up. Thematically again centring on relationships and people struggling to communicate – like much of this record – the instrumentation is absolutely sparse. It's easy to see Chris writing this on a simple acoustic. It's at this point that anyone looking for a drastic change of direction from Coldplay might have switched off, but they would surely have been chastised for a dramatic creative swerve at this point in their career.

'Low' is perhaps the record's most obvious 'U2' moment, dipping into psychedelia again but with its own slice of magnificence. You can almost hear it being performed at Red Rocks, whether it is Chris's high register, the chugging bass and workmanlike drums, or Jonny's simple but memorable riffing. Then, without warning, the next track, 'The Hardest Part', throws us straight into a scene where REM have become Chris Martin's backing band. The song's tapestry is rich in melody and hooks, as commercial as a rock band can get without turning into pure pop. By now the album is beginning to sound like one classic after another, sweeping along with an enviable momentum of hooks, emotion and bombast.

Next up is 'Swallowed In The Sea', the sibling song to 'Fix You', the band again unashamedly mining a rich balladic vein. Few groups could compete with Coldplay in this genre and *X&Y* reinforces the point. It would perhaps not have seemed out of place on *Parachutes*, but this is why Coldplay are – more than anything else – an *honest* band.

They can create a song that is this simple yet powerful and capture it without fuss or pretension. Coldplay are constantly criticised for being fey, wimpish, feeble – yet songs like 'Swallowed In The Sea' prove they are anything but.

Unfortunately the last 'listed' track, 'Twisted Logic', is a turgid plod through maudlin emotion. Chris's lyrics barely rise above the ordinary and the band sound like they have run out of energy. There's an effort at bringing matters to a majestic close, but it struggles to convince. It's easily the album's weakest moment. Following on from this disappointing nadir is the 'hidden track', 'Til Kingdon Come', the song the band wrote for the late Johnny Cash. It is so easy to hear Cash singing this and it is sad that he never did. Nevertheless, Chris does a sterling job and his voice is more than up to the task of accompanying this stripped-back strum-along. However, it certainly proves that when the band said they were Cash fanatics, they weren't simply name-dropping.

The album definitely has slightly rougher edges than its predecessor, although it's hardly Napalm Death. Nonetheless, the reverb-drenched, delayed guitar soundscapes of Jonny Buckland were very reminiscent of early The Edge and conjured visions of anthemic stadium shows and 100,000 cigarette-lighters/mobile phones being lifted into the air. Chris's piano work on the album was delicate yet powerful; he seemed able to choose exactly when a simple line would add to the melody and also know when to stay out of the spotlight. Some of the tracks were immediate classics – 'Fix You' becomes engrained in the brain after just one play, for example. The 'second' side is weaker, but the record still leaves the listener feeling that the band have achieved a watershed moment in their career.

Oasis's 1997 album, *Be Here Now*, was the only album to have sold over half a million copies in the first week of release in the UK, shifting a staggering 695,761 units. Dido's *Life For Rent* was some way behind in second place with first-week sales of 400,351. When the chart was announced at the end of the week in which *X&Y* was released, Coldplay were delighted to find that it had become the second fastest-selling album ever with a staggering 464,000 copies sold in less than seven days. Coincidentally, the band's third long player knocked Oasis's lacklustre latest offering, *Don't Believe The Truth*, from the top spot.

Even better news was yet to come. Over in America, where the band's momentum had been growing since the last record, the album topped the prestigious *Billboard* Top 200 album charts, a feat achieved by only a select clique of British bands. Sales figures there were even more mind-boggling, with nearly 750,000 copies sold in a week. Despite career-best first week sales for albums by The Black Eyed Peas, The White Stripes and Shakira, Coldplay topped the lot. They also had the biggest first-week US sales for any rock band since U2's *How To Dismantle An Atomic Bomb* the previous year. In contrast, despite going on to sell four million units Stateside, *A Rush Of Blood To The Head* had originally débuted with sales of 141,000. Meanwhile, *X&Y* stayed at the top of the US charts for three weeks, surpassing a million units in a month and eventually selling in excess of five million copies in that country alone. The 400,000 tickets for their 38-show North American tour sold out in one weekend.

The album also topped the charts in another 26 countries, including territories as diverse as Argentina, Chile, Hong Kong, Lebanon and Malaysia. However, it was not all positive. Despite their huge profile and chart success in the USA, two of the most prestigious critical publications were scathing about the new record. A negative *Rolling Stone* review was bad enough, but the review in *The New York Times* was vicious. The writer systematically derided the new record and was openly critical of the band's grandeur. It was a blisteringly negative piece that could be summed up by the line claiming they were "the most insufferable band of the decade". Chris admitted that these two pieces "knocked us sideways". The stellar sales and sell-out concert suggested that neither of these pieces had had much impact on the album's success. In the UK, there were few snipers, although later the band came second in a poll of BBC 6 Music listeners that proclaimed *X&Y* the second most over-rated album ever, second only to Nirvana's *Nevermind*.

Coldplay launched into an exhausting world tour to promote *X&Y*. Many bands of this size might appear at the key festivals – Coachella, Glastonbury, Isle of Wight, for example – and then play a smattering of the stadiums around the world. Not so Coldplay: they began with two warm-up shows in London and Paris before starting the ball rolling by heading off to Europe (with Richard Ashcroft as support), then back for two weeks of absurdly massive shows in the UK. On the last weekend in June, 2005, the band played arguably their most prestigious gig ever – a headline slot at Glastonbury. The previous two appearances had been a big success and Coldplay definitely felt they had an affinity with the famous festival. However, initially Chris told Michael Eavis that they might not be able to play the 2005 gig, until he was informed that there would be no festival in 2006 (a so-called fallow year to let the cows graze and the ground recover) and they instantly became available for 2005 after all.

The last time they had played, three years previously, few people in the crowd knew the new songs featured in their set. Now they were known – literally word for word – by *everyone*. Headlining the weekend was obviously an altogether different experience and one they will never forget. The grounds were considerably more wet and muddy than usual, due to torrential downpours. There had even been a power cut due to the inclement weather. This mattered not. Opening with 'Square One', the band played the gig of their lives, with Chris even altering the lyrics of 'Politik' to "Give me weather that does no harm/ Michael Eavis, Worthy Farm/Give me mud up to my knees/The best festival in history". During 'Speed Of Sound' Chris jested, 'Crazy Frog, where are you now?'. The soaring music and emotional lyrics almost seemed to lift people out of the knee-deep mud. Chris hinted that the band was having a difficult time behind the scenes with two vague comments: he dedicated their encore, a cover of Kylie's 'Can't You Get Out Of My Head', to "absent friends", and also said, "Things are a bit shit now but they'll be all right." The amazing rendition of 'The Scientist' was acknowledged by many as the stand-out moment of the entire weekend. Even Glastonbury legend Michael Eavis said Coldplay had been his highlight.

After he'd finished singing to the 100,000 Glastonbury faithful, Chris went home to visit his parents. And promptly got told off for not putting the milk away. Again.

With a triumphant Glastonbury behind them, Coldplay were actually only just beginning their travels. The six vast UK shows around this fortnight were punctuated by the two Live 8 gigs – global concerts to raise awareness of Third World debt and the 'Make Poverty History' campaign (with Bob Geldof at the helm). Coldplay appeared with Richard Ashcroft (following on from U2 no less) and Chris was clearly in buoyant mood: he introduced Ashcroft as "the greatest singer on Earth", said The Verve's 'Bittersweet Symphony' was "the best [song] ever written" and that the concerts were "'the greatest thing that's ever been organised in the history of the world". However, later Chris expressed his opinion that the band themselves could have performed better. "Richard Ashcroft was brilliant but I thought we were crap. Robbie Williams was absolutely amazing, so were Pink Floyd." Chris also criticised the numerous cynics who derided the weekend, pointing out (again) that there were bigger issues being promoted here.

Then it was back to the UK's biggest stadia again (in all they played Crystal Palace National Sports Centre twice, Bellahouston Park in Glasgow twice, and the Reebok Stadium in Bolton twice). Ever a band to provoke a reaction, in the same week that Queen said they disliked Coldplay because their songs "all sound the same", a resident of Kenley in Surrey complained to Bromley Council after the band's two-night stay at the National Sports Centre in Crystal Palace, claiming the sound of the concert was too loud – not an unusual complaint for a rock band on the surface, but surprising when you realise the gig was *nine miles* from his home. At first he had thought it was a neighbour's kids' band, but was outraged when he learned that it was actually the soft rock kings, who were clearly taking a leaf out of Black Sabbath's book on volume levels. Fourteen other people complained that night!

By now the band were performing in front of tens of thousands of people at each gig and their following was sufficiently large to require multiple nights at each venue. Organising this fell to a man widely regarded as the best tour manager in the business, Andy Franks, who has also taken Robbie Williams and Depeche Mode out on the road. When he began working with Coldplay, those in the industry knew that the band had officially graduated to genuine stadium-filling greatness.

For the band, the scale of the shows was not taken for granted. Jonny was open about his apprehensions: "The gigs have got really big. Almost too big. The temptation is to put in all the cheesy moves and run around and get down on your knees and shit. We try to do what we do – but just slightly bigger."

Next they went to Europe for three shows before boarding a plane to the USA, where a massive slew of huge autumn concerts awaited them, including two nights at Madison Square Garden. Nearly 30 enormodomes were visited before they returned for yet more European shows (including some big festivals) and then a further UK tour in December. The final UK arena dates headed towards a close with shows at London's cavernous Earl's Court, followed by Newcastle, Manchester and Belfast. However, many reviewers suggested the band needed more than just six weeks off before their next gigs, as their performances towards the end of these UK dates were frequently reviewed as "tired". Maybe it was the outrageous and bacchanalian activity in the dressing room before each show? Perhaps not, given that items on Coldplay's rider – the list of preferred items a band supplies to venues for each gig – were said to include, "48 cold lagers, six packs of Marlboro Lights and eight pairs of dark cotton socks size 9-11".

'Fix You' and 'Talk' were worthy second and third singles from the album during the closing months of 2005; they generously donated all proceeds from the US download of 'Fix You' to a fund to help victims of Hurricane Katrina, which had ripped the city of New Orleans apart with devastating brutality.

Unlike many bands, Coldplay openly enjoy the recording process and, although they are fans of playing live too, they certainly cherish the time spent creating new material in the studio. This didn't mean they were immune to criticism of their live shows however: support act Richard Ashcroft revealed that after some gigs on the tour the band huddled around a computer and logged on to the internet fan forums to see what people had thought of various sections of the shows.

Finally they were able to enjoy a welcome six-week break over Christmas of 2006, ahead of another colossal US tour starting in the New Year, which would encompass more than 30 US dates before they took more time off (a much-needed two-month break in April and May 2006). Rumours that Gwyneth was expecting a second child were fuelled by reports – unconfirmed – that her mother had mentioned she would soon become a grandmother for the second time. Spokesmen for the couple refused to confirm this and stated only that it was a private matter. Then, in December 2005, Gwyneth finally appeared to confirm that the rumours were true after all, in an off-the-cuff comment by fellow Hollywood star Orlando Bloom. The heart-throb had complimented her on the fullness of her buxom chest and she responded that it was "one of the best things about being pregnant".

Meanwhile, back out on the road – and probably to the horror of his security manager – Chris had developed a penchant for going to Coldplay gigs on public transport. Why? Because it put him in a bad mood and from that miserable atmosphere he felt he often pulled out some of his best live performances. He has been known to go to arenas full of Coldplay fans on the same train, or in the same traffic jam, and even queue for hot dogs outside the venue. "So I know just what it's like for everyone else who is paying. It makes me more determined to get onstage and really deliver a show that makes it all worthwhile for everyone."

One fun highlight of the spring 2006 US dates came in February in Anaheim, California when Chris suffered his very own 'wardrobe malfunction' after his trousers fell down mid-set. Without pausing for breath, Chris turned to where Gwyneth was seated in the VIP area and said, "You can only really get away with this if you've got an arse as good as Brad Pitt's." Then he immediately went into an improvised song about his own backside, while the rest of the band fell about laughing as they tried to provide impromptu musical backing to words such as, "It should never have come to pass that you caught sight of my ass".

Another hiccup on the US campaign occurred when they were forced to cancel two gigs due to a "throat illness" suffered by the singer. Expert doctors had been called upon and they advised that to continue without a brief respite might risk cancelling more concerts and, eventually, possibly endanger Chris's voice.

The tour was obviously gruelling and reports surfaced that the band were on the verge of splitting many times, although the reality was altogether a lot less dramatic. Will qualified these exaggerated rumours by explaining that they were simply "all getting on each other's tits at the moment".

It was a mark of Coldplay's American success that Chris duetted with REM's Michael Stipe on a charity EP during these dates to raise funds for the continuing efforts towards rehabilitating survivors of Hurricane Katrina. The duet of 'In The Sun' they performed together was used on an episode of *Grey's Anatomy* shortly after the Super Bowl, generally regarded as the premier television weekend in the American entertainment calendar.

Not a band to rest on their laurels, on the second leg of their US tour they still heavily promoted Oxfam's Big Noise Petition, which called upon world leaders to alter trading terms and conditions for the poorest nations. By the time it was delivered to world trade ministers in December at the WTO Ministerial Conference in Hong Kong, this petition would contain over 17 million signatures.

Having recently confirmed reports that she was expecting their second child during an interview at the Screen Actors Guild showing of her new film, *Proof*, in Beverly Hills, Gwyneth was on a flight from New York to Venice that was forced to make an emergency landing due to an engine fault. Although the descent was relatively stable, the crew did notify passengers of the predicament and, as the plane came in to land, fire engines and ambulances swarmed around the landing strip. Gwyneth was very unsettled by the trauma: "I thought, 'Oh, no, I'm not going out like this, surely? Please, not now.' It's only now that I see how unhappy and turbulent my twenties really were. There was everyone saying, 'Oh, aren't you lucky? You have a marvellous life.' And me thinking, 'If it is that marvellous, why do I feel so sad?' I cannot believe how my life has turned around. I have a great husband, a beautiful daughter, and another baby on the way. My life is full and so happy."

Not content with having already played most of Europe's and north America's biggest venues, Coldplay next headed to the southern hemisphere for yet more dates in Australasia, the Far East and Japan, taking the world tour right through to July 19, 2006, performing a final tired but happy show in Budokan, Japan. On the tour itself, the band didn't mind being wide-eyed and jet-lagged in the dead of night because for once they had something good on television to watch – the World Cup. The boys were football fans, and Will later became close friends with Portuguese legend Luis Figo. At the lower end of the football scale, Will also helped out AFC Totton, whose goalkeeper, Iain Brunnschweiler, used to jam on guitar alongside the future Coldplay drummer in that fledgling band Fat Hamster back when they were all only 13.

The band's only British gig of 2006 came at the Isle of Wight Festival in June. The band flew in by helicopter over the 60,000 revellers and were on the same bill as The Prodigy, Richard Ashcroft and Foo Fighters, among others. One notable live cover was their version of fellow performer Lou Reed's 'Perfect Day'. In jubilant mood, Chris even told the crowd that he would release a single called 'Do The Crouch' if England did well at the forthcoming World Cup – in honour of the star striker Peter Crouch and his trademark 'robot' dance. He also invited a female fan on stage to drink champagne with the band as 'crowd member of the year'.

Taking into account warm-up shows, festivals and their own headline dates, Coldplay performed in excess of 110 live shows around the launch of *X&Y*. Along the way, the massive world tour generated over $66 million, putting the band in the top 15 live acts. Later they were named 'Britain's Richest Band' ahead of The Rolling Stones, Paul McCartney and Elton John. *Heat* magazine's 'top earners' feature also posted Coldplay as having made £25.3 million in 2005, second only to

The Rolling Stones (although a *Rollingstone.com* 'rich list' put them at 23, albeit still ahead of the likes of Eminem, the Red Hot Chili Peppers, Radiohead and Sir Paul McCartney). Within six months of *X&Y* being released, EMI's coffers had swelled, with not only a sales boost from that massive album but also from further positive campaigns for Gorillaz, The Rolling Stones, Paul McCartney and KT Tunstall. This was due in no small part to *X&Y* selling over six million copies worldwide in the first month of release. Amazingly, despite the brilliant commercial success and no small number of rave reviews, *X&Y* was not the year's biggest release. That honour fell to blue blood James Blunt, whose *Back To Bedlam* album – fuelled by the mega-selling single 'You're Beautiful' – shifted 1,526,000 copies in the UK, a mere 2,000 more than Coldplay's effort.

With sales of *X&Y* eventually topping 10 million, even the ambitious Chris Martin would have been pleased with the album's success as his plane headed back over the Atlantic from New York towards London. Coldplay finally landed back home in the summer of 2006 with one thought on their minds (other than rest!): the next album... With rumours swirling of possible collaborations with Kanye West, Justin Timberlake, Beyoncé and Nelly Furtado, it seemed that Coldplay could work with almost anyone they wanted (Guy was not averse to his own collaborations too, with two outings alongside A-ha's Magne F, latterly on the album *A Dot Of Black In The Blue Of Your Bliss*). But what they wanted more than anything else was to start work on their next album.

CHAPTER 22

Drumsticks

"Matthew McConaughey's in his thirties, right, and there's absolutely no hair on his chest. How did that happen?"
            Chris Martin's final thought, after a Q&A with students
                        at the esteemed McCallum High School

"Chris Martin's Right Hand. 100% Genuine – Comes with Certificate of Authenticity. Ideal for signing CD Albums/Single/Posters etc. Don't miss your chance to own this rare limited stock. Only 100 available."
                        Ebay posting, January 2007

Coldplay's career at this point seemed to be a peculiar yet entertaining mixture: on the one hand, we have campaigning multi-millionaire superstars, flying around the world championing Fair Trade, asking awkward questions of evasive politicians and using their fame for the considerable benefit of a number of philanthropic issues. However, in contrast to these worthy efforts, the band was also beginning to appear in a number of much more light-hearted cameos, with interviews and appearances that at times were genuinely comic.

Chris Martin's peculiar mix of super-celebrity, bombast, self-deprecation and down-to-earth humility was in evidence once again during a strenuous series of live dates. He went from duetting with Michael Stipe and popping round to Madonna's house for a party with Gwyneth to making a cup of tea for Jules Segal, who was in the midst of a bizarre but fascinating project called 'Greeting The 500'. Segal was aiming to meet 500 celebrities in the last six months of 2006. Having already met Jonathan Ross and Neil Kinnock, among many others, Jules revealed how Chris seemed to go the extra mile: "Chris was an absolute star. I congratulated him on the recent announcement made by him and Gwyneth. We chatted about the bet and how I needed 100 handshakes to win it and how I only had about 50 with three weeks to go!" Chris actually went to his house to meet Jules!

In keeping with his clearly more self-aware and self-deprecating mindset, in the autumn of 2006 Chris appeared in the second series of *Extras*, the brilliant comedy by Ricky Gervais. The show is based around the exploits of the downtrodden film 'extra' Andy Millman (played by Gervais), who aspires to the limelight but remains in the shadow of various real-life celebrities – brilliantly caricatured by stars like David Bowie, Orlando Bloom, Robert De Niro and Kate Winslet, among many other star-studded names. In the second series, Millman has secured his own sitcom – *When The Whistle Blows* – but events begin to unravel as the show quickly becomes hugely popular. Millman begins to despair at the manipulation and shallowness of the television world and, by definition, his own life. It's yet another comedy masterclass from the man (along with Stephen Merchant) behind *The Office*.

In this particular episode, Andy Millman makes a video for charity and Chris Martin comes along to lend his famously supportive hand. However, Chris is quickly revealed as a shameless self-promoter. At the photo shoot to raise funds for African poverty, Chris asks the organisers if he can have a picture of the (fictitious) *Coldplay Greatest Hits* album cover next to a starving African child. When that request is refused, he asks if maybe one of the children could hold the CD, or perhaps play 'Trouble' in the background. Then as he poses for the photo, he unzips his jacket to reveal a *Greatest Hits* T-shirt. He then sweet-talks himself on to Millman's old-school sitcom about factory life in Wigan, much to Millman's horror. On the show, Coldplay perform 'Fix You'. Chris had ended the cameo at the earlier photo shoot by saying, "Can we get on with this, I've got to do AIDS and Alzheimer's and landmines this afternoon and I wanna get back for *Deal Or No Deal*, plus Gwyneth's making drumsticks."

Another clip, which was viewed by millions of Coldplay fans, was an interview with Gervais 'grilling' Chris on www.rickygervais.com. Gervais – himself arguably the world's biggest comedian by 2005 – did not shy away from the trickiest of questions. While Chris bounced between poker-faced acting, obvious discomfort at the staggeringly inappropriate questions and outright laughter when he was unable to control himself, Gervais played the deadpan interviewer perfectly. Ricky asked such deeply inappropriate questions as, "You like to buy clothes made in Third World sweatshops because they're cheaper. Do you prefer Chinese or Indian-made stuff?"; and, "You love getting corporate sponsorship for stuff, and you named your child Apple obviously after the computer firm. How much money did you get for that?"; and, "On tour, you have the band and tour in stitches with your famous impression of a disabled. Why do they find that so funny?"; plus, "You famously said you don't trust black people. Isn't that racist?" Chris is up to the challenge and is obviously having a blast.

The rest of the band were not averse to such antics either. Two years' previously, Chris and Jon had appeared on a spoof chat show with presenter Vernon Kaye to promote a new cause, Zombaid. With absolutely deadpan faces, they explain that Guy and Will have been bitten by zombies while orienteering and terminated – before even the band's management could help. They said that Guy's fingers were too fat to play afterwards but that Will could still play the drums "despite being dead". They also revealed that "Sting, Paul McCartney and Dr Fox" were also zombies. This tragedy had alerted them to the fact that zombies had few rights and so they had launched Zombaid to raise awareness of this issue. At the close of the interview, actors Simon Pegg and Nick Frost (stars of the hit movie *Shaun Of The Dead*, which this spoof was promoting and in which Chris made a brief cameo) are revealed as the new members of Coldplay. Then Chris finishes with the news that the next Coldplay tour will be sponsored by Asda and the band will be doing a corned beef promotion on the road. The official Zombaid website can be visited at www.zombaid.co.uk, where you can buy merchandise and help raise funds for this most serious of issues.

Despite the exhausting road trip to promote *X&Y*, Coldplay still experienced numerous light-hearted moments during the campaign. One bright fillip for Chris was receiving a famous (honorary) *Blue Peter* badge for his tireless campaigning for Make Trade Fair. He'd actually gone on the legendary kids' television show to present a badge to a 12-year-old boy who himself had campaigned for fair trade. Then the presenter surprised Chris with his own medal. "I've always wanted a criminal record and a *Blue Peter* badge – now I've got both."

As if to reinforce the band's ubiquity, when Apple announced that the one billionth download had been purchased by a man from Michigan, it was almost inevitably a Coldplay track, 'Speed Of Sound'. The customer won himself a 20-inch iMac, ten iPods and a $10,000 gift card in the process – not bad for a $0.79 download. Even more incredibly, it was reported that Apple were going to pay for a scholarship at the world-renowned Juilliard School of Music in this man's name to commemorate this milestone. Good job he hadn't downloaded 'Crazy Frog'.

In a development sure to have Liam Gallagher frothing at the mouth, Chris was declared the third most influential 'middle-class celebrity' by the 'Class Of 2006' survey (Jamie Oliver won for his school dinners campaign, although the fact that he was the son of a publican, went to government school and left with no qualifications seemed to have been missed). Later, when Chris was voted the 49th Most Powerful Person On The Planet, Gwyneth came in at 28th. At least he could savour the 'Sexiest Vegetarian' award he also won during this period. Probably best that no one told Liam Gallagher there was even talk of a 'Coldplay ballet'.

The awards season predictably doffed its cap to Coldplay again. In contrast to Oasis, who refused to attend the Brits because their latest album had not been nominated, Coldplay were nominated for 'Best Single' ('Speed Of Sound'), 'Best Group', 'Best Live Act' and 'Best British Album'. And at last Coldplay fans had some news about the next record: this time, reinventing the wheel wasn't going to be enough as they were aiming to create "the greatest piece of music ever made". At least this is what Chris told reporters at the pre-Brits party, although those present were hard put to hear what he was saying due to his tongue being planted very firmly in his cheek.

On the night, the band (who were no fans of award ceremonies and never afraid to say as much) won 'Best British Album' and 'Best British Single'. Confounding the critics, who called him arrogant for his lofty proclamations prior to the previous album's release, Chris accepted the awards and said, "It is hard for us sometimes because we are English and we do not like to admit we are great. So tonight, we would like to agree with you for giving us this award." Mysteriously, he went on to say, "People are fed up with us and so are we", before adding, "Thanks for having us, you won't see us for a long time." Cue worldwide panic on every Coldplay fansite. Worse still, the beleaguered EMI share price fell by 3% the next day as anxious investors worried that one of the label's crown jewels was about to disband (however, it quickly recovered). Not that Chris ever actually said they were disbanding, but in the markets, sentiment is everything.

Back on the awards trail, they received three Grammy nominations without winning a prize, and there were also nods from the Mercury Music Prize and the Ivor Novellos (where they received three nominations, for 'International Hit Of The Year' and 'Most Performed Work' with 'Speed Of Sound, and for 'Best Song' with 'Fix You'). Notably, early supporter *NME* had long since stopped nominating the band at its own annual award ceremony.

Coldplay's overwhelming success – both commercially and critically – reflected a growing trend of guitar-based music overtaking pop as the predominant genre in the British music scene during the middle of the decade. Aside from their own massive success, the likes of Kaiser Chiefs, Oasis, Keane and KT Tunstall also enjoyed bumper years. The overseas winners were also mainly rock bands, with the likes of Green Day, Foo Fighters and The Killers all achieving sizeable sales. This was particularly encouraging during a time of growing concerns over download culture, which many had predicted would pull the plug on developing new long-term talent. With bands enjoying most of their income from live performances, the digital revolution seemed to have placed more emphasis on artists who could actually deliver the goods onstage, and this in turn had re-energised the rock genre, after years of taking second place in a pop-dominated world.

Chris's headline grabbing Brits speech was probably long overdue. In terms of time off, the band had been relentlessly working and playing live for two years and, although the third album campaign had cemented their reputation as a band of global status, they were due a break. In classically obtuse fashion, when asked by *The Daily Mirror* at an EMI party why the band were going on an extended sabbatical, Chris said, "You know, if the fox stays in the hole for too long it might get shot. Sometimes the fox needs to get back into its hole." This self-imposed exile was inevitably reinterpreted by some as the beginning of the end for the band, with rumours even circulating that Chris had already quit Coldplay. These rumours were then replaced by speculation about a five-year hiatus, which was also just plain wrong. However, it would be many months before the British public heard either another recorded or live note from the Coldplay camp.

CHAPTER 23

The Fabulous Baker Boys

"I heard a Bono quote once that said, 'Bands shouldn't break up over money, they should break up over track listing'."
Chris Martin, prior to the release of the band's fourth album

Although the band was inactive for an unusually long time between July 2006 and February 2007, this period of apparent quietude was actually anything but. On a personal level, the years 2006 and 2007 were a hive of new developments. Jonny Buckland married his long-time girlfriend, Chloe Lee-Evans, and, in typically low-key fashion, quietly confirmed this when approached by a reporter as he left a New York restaurant. In November 2007, they welcomed their first child, a daughter named Violet, which Guy's wife, Jo, had revealed in *The Guardian*. Will and his teacher wife, Marianne, also celebrated the arrival of a baby girl, named Ava-Mae, in early May 2006. A month before, Chris and Gwyneth had welcomed their second child, Moses Martin, to a predictable press frenzy due to the so-called 'superstar parents', as the tabloids were wont to christen them. Reportedly 'Moses' was the name of a song Chris penned for his wife in 2003. Then in September that same year, Guy and Jo welcomed the birth of their daughter, whom they named Nico. A rare glimpse into the couple's life came with an unusually insightful article in *The Sunday Telegraph*, during which Guy's designer wife showed the paper around their home.

One other personal anecdote of note occurred when Chris bumped into an old school associate who had bullied the Coldplay singer for being a "swot" and derided him for preferring music over sports. This person had constantly told Chris he would "make nothing of himself". So it was perhaps understandable that when Chris saw him in a London street one day, the Coldplay frontman was for once more than happy to say hello, ask after what he was doing and introduce him to his wife, the Hollywood superstar Gwyneth Paltrow.

Of course, on a professional level, Coldplay had a new record to make. As 2007 began, the band looked back on what had been a particularly quiet year for their British fans, and Guy offered some encouraging news about the evolution of the new album. "We hope to have something together by January 2007," he told one magazine. "We're going to make sure with our new album that everyone remembers why Coldplay are one of the best bands in the world." A month earlier Chris had performed four songs at a charity gig, including two Dylan covers, a Killers track and a 'new' Coldplay song called 'Bucket For A Crown'. Apart from some South American dates at the start of the year, the band rarely broke cover to play live in 2007, although most notably they did appear at the soon-to-be-annual series of shows under the banner of Live Earth, designed to raise awareness of climate change.

Back in the studio, although there was no talk this time of "reinventing the wheel", Guy was quick to suggest that they were still looking to break the Coldplay mould. "It's been said before that we really view these first three albums as part of a trilogy and it's now time to move on. We feel that we don't really have to prove ourselves any more to people and that gives you an amazing amount of creative freedom to do stuff." What they were definitely *not* going to do was invite the same large number of people into the creative process that they had during the *X&Y* sessions. At times, there had been over 50 different people in the studio or commenting on the sessions and that was not something they intended to repeat. "I don't want to listen to 55 people next time we record. We went through a period of believing everyone. I literally listened to the tea boys last time."

Unlike the transient – and protracted – sessions for the third album, this time Coldplay quickly became focused on their new recording. Initial plans were made to either build or buy their own studio. Eventually they hired a disused, white-fronted bakery in Primrose Hill, north-west London, which Chris deliberately chose because of its nondescript exterior. It was hidden away down an alley, opposite a housing estate. "I used to walk past it every day," he told *NME*, "and think, 'What an ugly place'. Then, one day, a 'To Let' sign appeared outside. I thought, 'Hmmm, that place is so ugly, I bet no one would bother us if we moved in there'." The scene was set. Then, within what seemed no time at all, the band were talking of already having written an album's worth of new material. For a band with such a tortuous studio history, could it really be that simple?

The news started to trickle out that the new Coldplay album was now not only ahead of schedule but almost complete. At the production helm was the legendary Brian Eno, who had been an original member of Roxy Music but later became a production icon, having famously worked with acts like U2 and David Bowie. Coldplay were openly delighted to be working with such a prestigious name: "Well, we kind of more feel that he picked us really. With someone like Brian, if you can persuade him to work with you, you're doing well." Initially Chris had only asked Eno if he knew of a producer who might like to work with them, rather than directly asking Eno himself. Then once they were working together, Eno wasted no time in giving it to the band straight: "He goes, 'Your songs are too long. And you're too repetitive, and you use the same tricks too much, and big things aren't necessarily good things, and you use the same sounds too much, and your lyrics are not good enough.' He broke it down." In the studio alongside Eno was the brilliant pairing of Markus Dravs (who'd also worked with Arcade Fire, a band Coldplay openly revered) and Rik Simpson, meaning they had a top-notch team at the helm.

Eno told *Music Week* that, "They want to take their music somewhere else. We're really at the very beginning of it, but it sounds very promising to me." When Chris finally commented on the new record, he seemed to have regained his (fragile) optimism, telling *NME* that, "In order for us to get excited about a new album, we have to have one song that we feel like everybody had to hear before we die, otherwise we'll be terribly depressed. So luckily with this new record we're going to make, we have that one song."

Life in the studio was extremely creative. Sometimes the more liberal morning recording sessions would devolve into free-form jazz improvisation. One of the more unusual methods was using 'magic cards'. Eno presented the band with cards, each with phrases on them such as 'play it backwards' or 'make it simpler', and they would randomly turn them over to see if that triggered any ideas.

As a teasing precursor, in March 2007 the band released a completist's dream box set, comprising every single A- and B-side, even including *The Blue Room EP*. But what fans really wanted to hear was the new album... there was just time for one more missed heartbeat at EMI when an April Fool's prank article on the internet announced the exclusive shock news that Chris Martin had split Coldplay up, and was leaving to start a business growing watermelons. The fictitious piece mentioned their biggest hit to date as 'Ode To Deodorant' and quoted Chris as saying, "The weight of making a fourth album was getting too much, with the record label wanting to put out a greatest hits to ease its financial pressure." For those who hadn't yet guessed it was all a hoax, the piece ended by saying, "There was nobody from EMI Records to answer the phone because it's a Sunday."

Sadly there was one actual split within the camp, when Guy and Jo separated in May 2007. Although reports suggested that the split was "amicable", it was nonetheless understandably devastating for both parties.

The band's own postings on their official website gave enlightening insights into the tense yet creatively productive sessions for the fourth album. Chris in particular found the tension difficult at times, but he openly acknowledged that this cut-and-thrust was the catalyst for much of their finest material. It was also revealed that the band would all gather for lengthy meetings – sometimes four or five hours long – during which they analysed in minute detail the progress of each song. These meetings were held with Coldplay's four members, plus Phil Harvey, Brian Eno and Markus Dravs. Unfortunately, some media outlets carefully edited certain quotes from Chris to imply that – yet again, apparently – the band were on the very verge of splitting up. Some even went so far as to suggest that, due to the fragile and fractious atmosphere in the studio, the band had scrapped the entire album. Not so, although it has to be said that by now only the most gullible of observers would take announcements about Coldplay splitting up with anything other than a large pinch of salt.

A series of studio stills and a short video were also posted on the official website, and the fanbase speculated about apparent 'hidden' messages that may have been contained within these images. Chris appeared to be making hand signals that were analysed as pronouncing the words 'Viva La Vida' and some lip-reading Coldplay fans (now there's a sub-genre!) confirmed that this was what Will also appeared to be mouthing. Elsewhere on the web, the band's Twitter page would soon have in excess of 750,000 followers.

One odd conspiracy centred around a Coldplay plate and mug, with some fans claiming there was even a hidden message here, with the words 'Jonny's Solo On 42' on the plate. According to reports, this meant there was a track called '42' on the forthcoming album and/or the new record was 42 minutes long. Apparently…

The fascination with 'conspiracy' that the band seem to generate is perhaps a surprising aspect of the Coldplay fanbase, especially as the band are often criticised for being 'soft rock', the sort of group who appeal to the listener who buys two albums a year and goes to Eighties revival gigs. In other words – by some odd, snobbish yardstick – not a 'proper' fan. Yet, this was clearly not the case: the various fan sites always had dense forums riddled with chat and speculation, detailing conspiracies surrounding new tracks, the meaning of artwork and such like, all further evidence that the band's fans were far more than simple fair-weather supporters.

As an aside, their website blog had by now become a vital source of first-hand, almost real-time information on the band's recording sessions and was heavily subscribed to by millions of fans worldwide – indicative of the way the internet had become a direct filter between bands and their fans, cutting out the conventional print and TV/radio media. Given that Chris had made no secret of his dislike of the media, this opportunity to literally talk *direct* to the band's fans was seized with some gusto. As the sessions progressed, the posts became steadily more buoyant and positive, and eventually there were real signs that the band – even the famously self-critical Chris Martin – were beginning to believe that they were in the process of creating something very special. Chris regularly trumpeted the talents of Brian Eno and Markus Dravs, and clearly felt privileged to be working with them.

Sessions transferred for a while to Barcelona and perhaps inevitably aspects of the new material began to resonate with a Spanish and Latin American influence. The band had also spent so much time the previous year playing vast shows in Argentina, Chile, Brazil and Mexico. Among the Barcelona sessions, the band even recorded some group vocals in churches, in search of not only a "change of scene" but also a different acoustic result.

Speaking to *Rolling Stone*, Chris was clearly excited about what was happening in the studio. He responded to a question about the impact of digital downloads on the validity of bands still releasing an entire long player (when fans could just download the best two or three tracks) by saying, "We think it's all about quality over quantity now, because there's so much noise everywhere, there's no point in putting anything out unless it's fucking amazing. I still think there's incredible merit in making albums, pieces of work that are the same length as Beethoven's symphonies used to be. There's something pleasing about that amount of music from one artist."

The band even dabbled with hypnotism according to comments made by Chris in Q magazine: "Everything over this past few months has been about taking off any shackles. We feel like we have so much to prove and so many ideas that we'd like to try – sometimes you need a hypnotist to give you the bravery to do it." And he said, it was "fun and interesting". Eno himself challenged them to use different recording methods from the previous three albums and emphasised that this record was influenced as much by the live experience as anything else. Eventually, news filtered out that mixing was due to be finished by Christmas 2007, with a tentative release date pencilled in for some time in the summer of 2008. One speculative title was *Prospekt*. As it transpired, the record's complex nature meant mixing continued well into February, and a final official release date of June 2008 was announced.

The first snippet of the new album was heard in the late spring of 2008. One night the *NME* editor received a phone call from Chris Martin, who was in the band's studio. He said he had just written "the perfect song" and wanted to get it out to *NME* readers somehow. So it was agreed that the very first taste of the new album would in fact be free, in the form of a 7" vinyl strapped to the cover of that magazine's May 7 issue. The song was 'Violet Hill' and for one week it was also available to download free of charge from the Coldplay website.

The track was a confident stomp of a single. There were more pseudo-religious backing vocals, but combined here with decidedly jagged and distorted guitars. Opening with an obviously Eno-influenced ambient soundscape, the track is jaunty and polished, with hints of The Beatles and even Echo & The Bunnymen in Chris's vocal. Only in the closing 30 seconds do Coldplay strip the tune back to a simple piano and the trademark Chris Martin vocals. Chris revealed that the opening lyric of 'Violet Hill' was actually the first line Coldplay ever wrote; indeed, it was apparently the line that convinced Guy Berryman to join the band. Once the accompanying album was released, it would transpire that this more experimental and strutting track was not particularly indicative of the record, but it served its purpose, pricking the ears of both Coldplay fans and those who were still to be converted.

The commercial reaction to 'Violet Hill' was very strong, with over two million people downloading the free track within days of its availability. Had the track been eligible for the official charts, it would have outsold the entire Top 40 *four times over.* (This wasn't the most important new arrival of 2008 for Will, however. On May 7, his wife gave birth to twins, a girl and boy named Juno and Rex, welcome siblings to Ava-Mae who was now two years old.)

All eyes were now on the album's summer launch. Amazingly, a full week before the release, the band streamed the entire record on their Myspace page, another example of their innovative approach to promoting their material. This was in part a reaction to the inevitable string of leaks, which fortunately did little to damage the new record's overall success. The band were also pleased to learn that the new long player was i-Tunes' most pre-ordered album ever. The Myspace strategy was also indicative of way the record business was now viewing the internet. Whereas previously the industry had sued its consumer – never a great idea – now the music biz had finally acclimatised itself to the new landscape, meaning clever PR campaigns such as this were more commonplace.

The new album was called *Viva La Vida*, although it was also given the 'alternative' title of *Death And All His Friends*. It transpired that the album's title had been chosen way back in March 2007. Chris had come across the phrase when reading about the Mexican artist Frida Kahlo. The band visited Frida's house while touring South America, as Will told BeQueen.de, "We visited Frida Kahlo's house and encountered this quote. We love Kahlo's art and were speechless in the face of the energy of the house, where the magnificent, expressive colours give a very special atmosphere. At this time we realised that we were too monotonous. We wanted to go away from black and white towards colour." The phrase means 'Live Life', although the exact Mexican translation would be 'Long Live Life'. The band admitted that the 'second' title was in part an attempt to divert attention away from the inevitable comparisons with Latino love-god Ricky Martin's famous 'Livin' La Vida Loca' song. Chris explained that the dual title was indeed deliberate: if fans were feeling optimistic, they could call it *Viva La Vida*, but if their mood was more somber, then the alternative *Death And All His Friends* was there too.

Once again the new album's artwork was fascinating, featuring a classic painting by the French Romantic artist Eugène Delacroix from 1830 called 'Liberty Leading The People'. The woman in the centre of the composition represents Liberty in the French Revolution, as she proudly holds the Tricolour above her head. The original painting sits in the Louvre in Paris (in 1999, the Japanese rock band Dragon Ash used a parody of this image for their own album, *Viva La Revolution*). On the album's sleeve notes there are numerous gaudy pictures and scribbled pieces of writing, again courtesy of Tappin Gofton. It wasn't just the recording sessions and writing that were stripped back: the band were also intricately involved in the design of the sleeve artwork, photography (Guy is co-credited with sleeve photography) and even the militaristic uniforms that the band wore on stage during the world tour to promote the album. Johnny later suggested that the band hand-stitched the uniforms themselves! As if to gently remind us that, despite all the hype and expectation, Coldplay were still keen to enjoy themselves, the sleeve notes comically hinted at the numerous locations used during the creation of the new album, telling us it had been recorded "in a bakery, a nunnery, a magic shop, a church".

Coldplay's fourth studio album begins with what the band do best – simple but grandiose music. The instrumental 'Life In Technicolor' (the US spelling is in fact correct because 'Technicolor' is a patented technology, and it's not that Coldplay were pandering to their US market as some misinformed observers have suggested) warmly introduces the listener to the album. Although the band had always intended to open this record with an instrumental, 'Life In Technicolor' had initially been written as a full-length song with lyrics. At one point the song was put to one side, but was resurrected and became the perfect cinematic opener. It's effectively a mini-overture driven by synths, military drums, timpani, joyously strummed guitars and the distant 'whoa-whoa' backing vocals, which of course make it instantly recognisable as Coldplay. There are also a few sparse electro-riffs that remind the listener that Brian Eno is sitting in the production chair. Chris typically had a more light-hearted explanation: "The reason we wanted to start this record with an instrumental is to: A) do a good ringtone, which is what that song is, and B) not have to have too much singing everywhere. By your fourth album, people are sort of bored with the singer's voice, you know." Jesting aside, this is an emotionally charged opener to a highly anticipated record.

The second track, 'Cemeteries Of London', finds the band stepping back in time to a dark, infested Victorian alleyway. The minor key dominates for the first 30 seconds before the tempo picks up, aided by some distinctly The Edge-esque riffing from Jonny. The song builds, layer upon upon layer, until by the close it sounds more like a triumphant religious chant than the decrepit and seedy whisper it began life as. The hand-claps and 'la-la-la' backing vocals ensure the atmosphere isn't too creepy, but a sinister undercurrent still remains. Lyrically, Chris delves into witches, night creatures, curses and ghosts, a murky subtext well suited to the rather schizophrenic track. The song closes with a simple piano riff, repeated once, thus neatly returning to its minimalist origins.

One of the first songs the band worked on for the new album was the third track, 'Lost!'. This is a lyrical high point of the album but, unfortunately, a musical dead end. Displaying obvious religious influences, the track skirts too closely to the bombastic. The hand-claps and preacher-like vocals, backed by the blatantly church-organ chords, are quite pedestrian, and even Jonny's simple but appealing guitar riff fails to lift the track out of the ordinary. The band revealed that they had been listening to 'Sing' by Blur, taken from their 1991 début *Leisure*, but Albarn's psychedelic track was far superior, opening with a stabbing melancholic piano and backward guitars. The phased keyboards and drum samples filled out the song with further Sixties atmosphere. It was an excellent, even daring ballad, unexpected from Blur, who at the time were perceived as essentially a pop band. By comparison, apart from some precise lyrics by Chris, the mildly entertaining sway of 'Lost!' seems cumbersome.

The next track, '42', the number that had been so speculated upon, is thankfully a return to form. It's classic Coldplay, opening with simple piano, melancholic Martin vocals, simple instrumentation reminiscent of 'The Scientist' and some of the band's finest string accompaniment to date. Then just before the song's halfway mark it suddenly explodes into a gargantuan crescendo. The disjointed and atonal guitars sound like a Radiohead and Free mash up, but then suddenly they change yet again through a brilliant melody hook. It's three songs in one, with the finale leading it back to Martin's super-fragile vocals. It's the album's first stand-out classic. Chris told *The New York Times* that, "That song is kind of a microcosm [of the entire album]. The lyrics in the beginning are very much big themes, but then we go into this kind of silly jam we wrote one day when we were all hypnotised, and then it ends with this big, up-tempo, positive thing. I don't know if it's any good, but it definitely captures everything in one place."

'Lovers In Japan/Reign Of Love' is pure stadium rock crafted by the genre's experts, filled with cascading keyboards and throbbing drums. Opening with echoes of U2-style guitar, the song then introduces rapid guitar strumming that echoes The Lotus Eaters' Eighties pop classic 'The

First Picture Of You'. It is arguably the album's finest production, and Eno manages to make a clean, sparse arrangement sound *enormous*. There is no clutter, anything that might be superfluous has been discarded. The closing moments of 'Lovers In Japan' build beautifully to an epic climax. It was easy to envisage Chris running around stages the world over, effortlessly orchestrating thousands of fans. Then suddenly it changes to 'Reign Of Love', which could easily have been played by Chris on a piano many years ago in Camden's The Falcon. Little insight has been given as to why these two tracks should have been paired up in such a way.

The next track is the longest on the record. At over seven minutes it's not clear if 'Yes' was christened as a tribute to the prog-rock legends of the same name. With Chris singing in an unusually low register, it sounds a little stunted, and is perhaps the album's weakest moment. Although he is lamenting a relationship, and the Middle Eastern strings momentarily excite, the second half kicks in awkwardly – yet another song with multiple personalities. After a brief pause around the four-minute mark, the guitar effects and winsome vocals make for a far better sonic backdrop, coupled with a punching drum line and shoe-gazing flavour that My Bloody Valentine would have been proud of. Just as with 'Lovers In Japan/Reign Of Love', however, the dual parts don't seem entirely connected, and on first listen they risk sounding like separate tracks. Nonetheless, it's a brave song, experimental and quirky, for which the band deserve credit. Perhaps Rick Wakeman was on the studio stereo after all?

The title track comes next, a clear highlight and one of the band's greatest moments (it would later win them numerous awards when released as a single). The beautiful string stabs were instantly recognised as one of *the* great song openings. It's one of those songs that sounds like it has always existed.

Chris's protagonist is the king of paranoia here, confused by the poisoned chalice that his days of privilege provide. The regal reflections on life that his lyrics ponder only add to the sense of grandeur, and the majestic additional instrumentation – timpanis, more strings, twinkling keyboards – just build and build until the song could not possibly get any more epic. This is classic Coldplay and possibly their best song ever.

'Violet Hill' is the album's most aggressive and darkest moment, but doesn't jar with its softer musical siblings. It's one of a number of tunes that benefitted from the electric violin (the Violectra) of Davide Rossi, who could also be heard playing with astounding prowess on 'Life In Technicolor', 'Lovers In Japan', 'Cemeteries Of London', '42', 'Yes' and 'Strawberry Swing'. Following 'Violet Hill', we reach the closing songs of this surprising and rewarding album. Penultimate (listed) track, 'Strawberry Swing', is a slice of genius. The intricate Afro-centric guitars would have appealed to fans of world music like Johnny Marr, who would also have enjoyed the obvious Beatles reference in the use of the word 'strawberry' backed up by a Sixties feel, particularly in Chris's vocal delivery. Yet again there is a stark change of direction midway, but at least on this occasion the band manages to convince the listener that it is part of the same song, rather than two distinct musical bedfellows forced together. Another production highlight, it again proves that Eno is a master at controlling a song through what he chooses to exclude rather than what he uses. It's restrained, beautiful and compelling.

The last listed track is the 'half-title' track, 'Death And All His Friends'. This hefty song opens with an almost Hall & Oates piano-led vibe, but soon evolves into another classic stadium monster. Eno introduces brilliant keyboards and layers of very subtle backing, alongside Elton John-like Seventies piano stabs, before Jonny delivers his finest guitar moment on the record, searing out his line while Chris sings behind him in multi-layered gospel vocals. It's a huge ending to the album and a stomping, triumphant stadium killer.

Then, after a pause, there comes the album's 'hidden' track – 'The Escapist' – which surprises and delights with its fabulous near-instrumental charms. Chris sings along quietly, but it is the minimalist and addictive keyboard motifs that impress. It's a beautiful ending to a memorable album, one racked by Martin's insecurities and encompassing the over-arching themes of life, love and death. It is not as complete a record as *X&Y*, and it certainly isn't as obviously commercial, but then perhaps that was part of the design. For all its moments of weakness – of which there are only really a smattering – *Viva La Vida* is, above all, an *honest* record.

CHAPTER 24

"Have We Cracked It Yet?"

Critical response to the new album was generally positive. Writing for *NME*, Mark Beaumont initially appeared on the verge of lambasting the band, but actually what he was saying was entirely positive: "They yearn to be recast as outsiders violently opposed to the mainstream hegemony but can't see that by dint of their incessant knack for a stadium-sized chorus they're so deeply entrenched in the mainstream that they're our men on the inside, making the most offensive indie racket palatable to the masses with a sprinkle of their melodic fairy dust." *Spin* magazine called the record, "a bold creative leap forward… while *X&Y* demonstrated Martin's knack for imbuing the everyday with grandeur, this consistently thrilling effort fills a much larger sonic canvas with much larger ideas". There were a few notable exceptions. Where previously *The New York Times* had lampooned the band, this time *The Independent*'s Andy Gill sharpened his pen for a venomous piece that among other criticisms called them, "pompous, mawkish, and unbearably smug". Elsewhere he reserved special disdain for Eno, saying, "One can only wonder how many muscle-bound oafs were required to carry the cheque that persuaded Eno to produce Coldplay's new album. I mean, given his rarefied cultural tastes, surely it can't have been the project highest on Eno's wish-list?" Interestingly, a blog on *The Independent*'s own website shortly after was entitled 'Why Andy Gill Was Wrong About Coldplay'.

Of course, the band was largely immune by now to the critic's pen. The album was a number one smash hit all around the world. In the UK, despite only being released midweek, the album sold over 300,000 copies, placing it among the fastest selling in chart history. By the summer, it would become the most downloaded album ever in the UK.

Next up was the album's title track, which was disqualified from charting when it was released as the second single in the early summer of 2008, because it had been available as a download to anyone pre-ordering the digital version of the new album. Once that offer had expired however, the single was instantly eligible for charting. This prolonged gestation eventually gave Coldplay their first ever UK number one single. With the corresponding album still at number one that week (outselling Duffy at number two by six to one), it was a magnificent double achievement for the band. Furthermore, in the same week, 'Violet Hill' was at number 11, and three other tracks ('Lost', 'Fix You' and 'Yellow') also re-entered the Top 100 chart listings (the album's chart success was reinforced when the single 'Lost!' also sold well).

The new album's success was again replicated in the USA, with the album and the forthcoming singles all doing superbly well. 'Viva La Vida' became their most successful US single, climbing to number three in the *Billboard* charts, eclipsing the previous best of number eight for 'Speed Of Sound'. The album débuted at number one; in the first week, the band sold more than 721,000 albums (only 16,000 behind the first week of fellow chart-topper *X&Y*), with over 300,000 of those sold on the very first day. Two weeks later, it was announced that *Viva La Vida* had already sold more downloads than any other album, recording over one million sales. Elsewhere the album topped the iTunes chart in countless territories, with the single following suit, while the physical CD topped the charts in 36 countries. It was a comprehensive domination of the global charts.

And how did Chris Martin celebrate these amazing feats in the press interviews of the time? Largely by injecting even more comedy into the proceedings than usual. One of his more bizarre interview statements concerned his concept of the perfect band. He revealed that he had been dreaming vividly about Radiohead and Westlife on consecutive nights. "That's the perfect blend of what we are trying to do…" He wasn't joking, apparently. Elsewhere he said he was disappointed that so few Coldplay songs were included on karaoke machines and in karaoke lyric books. "If we could just get eight in every bar worldwide I'd be happy. I would know we've made it. I think there are three karaoke possibilities on *Viva La Vida*. It surely has to be the ultimate measure of success."

Guy ran the London Marathon in April 2008, but if Coldplay's usual tour cycle was anything to go by, his endurance efforts were only just starting. Once again the band visited arenas all over the world on a vast global tour that was exhaustive in its coverage. Unlike a string of American acts that had begun to fly to the UK merely to play a multi-night residency at the O2, Coldplay travelled to all corners of each country. A couple of very small breaks aside, the world tour saw them playing multiple gigs every single month from the album's release through the rest of 2008, all of 2009 and well into the spring of 2010. The previous world tour had taken in approximately 150 dates and this jaunt looked like being no different.

Interestingly, Will revealed that the band did not take months to rehearse for live shows, mainly because they had already put in the work a long time ago. "We find out how a song should sound in order to let it work live," he told the website www.tagesanzeiger.ch, "but we don't spend months with rehearsals before a tour. This [preparatory work] happens before we go into the studio. During this time, we rehearse the songs, discarding ideas and work meticulously on details."

There were many notable shows along the way, most obviously the free gigs at London's Brixton Academy (presented live by Radio 1, still heavy-hitting champions of the band as it had been since their early days); there were also free concerts at New York's Madison Square Garden and in Barcelona's Espacio Movistar. Tickets for these shows were only available to lucky competition winners. After the Brixton gig they also performed for a select audience at BBC Television Centre.

Another obvious tour highlight was their appearance outside, in the streets of New York, at the Rockefeller Plaza for the Toyota Concert Series and *The Today Show*, where absolute joyous chaos ensued. Several streets in NYC had to be shut down as thousands of fans descended on the venue. Their performance was at the ungodly hour of just after 8.30am, but was nevertheless witnessed by thousands of frantic fans, enjoying a rare chance to see their heroes up close.

The live show was a massive operation and once again the band relied on the legendary tour manager Andy Franks to shepherd them around the world's biggest venues. The set list was eclectic, with even some of the more obtuse tracks from the album, such as 'Lost!', being aired and sounding very strong.

Despite Coldplay having been around the world many times, despite the thousands of road miles and countless anonymous hotels they had visited, the band was still essentially that merry band of troubadours that Simon Williams had witnessed way back in the late Nineties. As Guy explained to timesleader.com, "I don't get nervous any more. But I still get that great sense of excitement. I love that moment right before we go on, that anticipation of the lights coming down. It never tires for me."

The inevitable dilemma for a huge band who wish to make their shows feel 'intimate', particularly for those people right at the back of the vast stadiums, was confronted on this tour by Coldplay reappearing in a venue's more remote parts to perform acoustic segments. This worked brilliantly, with the band's breath taken away by both the joy of the fans they surprised and also the cavernous sing-along party atmosphere such a neat trick engendered.

By contrast, Jonny refreshingly said, "Do we miss the intimacy of small shows? In all honesty, no. We do occasionally do smaller shows, where you can see what people are ordering to drink. Those gigs are absolutely terrifying for us. When you take away all the stage set, we feel naked."

One interesting occurrence during this mammoth world tour was a 'side project' for Guy entitled Apparatjik. Working with A-Ha's Magne Furuholmen and also Jonas Bjerre, their track 'Ferreting' was included on the soundtrack for the BBC television show *Amazon*, which detailed adventurer Bruce Parry's exploits in the South American jungle basin. Some way north of the Amazon, the Frida Kahlo Museum in Mexico reported a substantial increase in visitor numbers since the Coldplay album had been released.

A neat April Fool's prank was posted in 2009, while the band was out on the road, when they announced that they were attempting to become the first group to record in zero gravity. They were 'reported' as having built a modified Boeing 727 with a studio inside and were planning to follow the astronaut-training programme, in which the plane climbs to high altitude only to nosedive at a vast speed. During this time a zero gravity field is created for about 25 seconds. Custom-made 'heavy' microphones would be needed to capture the unique studio sessions. Chris was even quoted as saying, "We've been searching for the right environment to record the perfect snare drum sound for many years now and I've just got a gut feeling that zero gravity is the place to do that."

Pushing the boundaries once again, the band also gave away a free concert CD on parts of this tour. *Left Right Left Right Left* was made available as a free digital download in May 2009, with actual physical copies also being given to those going to non-festival gigs on the remaining dates of the *Viva La Vida* tour. Immediately, Coldplay attracted criticism from smaller bands, whose concern was that only the ultra-wealthy groups could afford to give away live music. Once again, Coldplay seemed damned if they did and damned if they didn't.

An unpleasant development came when news broke that the band were embroiled in a legal dispute with the guitarist Joe Satriani, who contested that elements of the track 'Viva La Vida' were very similar to his 2004 composition 'If I Could Fly'. Coldplay denied the accusations with the following statement: "If there are any similarities between our two pieces of music, they are entirely coincidental, and just as surprising to us as to him. Joe Satriani is a great musician..." Later, Chris said that after the initial shock, he had tried to turn the experience into a positive, saying it had inspired him to write even more amazing songs. The case was eventually resolved with an 'order upon stipulation' with the two parties coming to a settlement, details of which remained private, but it was made clear that Coldplay did not have to admit to any wrong-doing.

The world tour continued relentlessly through 2009: that year's run of gigs seemed to take in the biggest venues in any country where a band can play. Support for the 2009 summer UK stadium shows came from an unlikely but welcome pop corner, Girls Aloud, whose Cheryl Cole had become the UK's most popular female celebrity. Chris admitted later that he personally called each member of the best-selling girl group to ask if they would come on tour with his band.

The Coldplay stadium show was not as vast as the famed U2 or Pink Floyd extravaganzas, but the band were not pretending to vie with such rock behemoths anyway. There was the usual assortment of large screens – an inevitable necessity for such big shows – as well as hundreds of giant balloons, massive sparklers and vintage TV sets. But this was stadium rock on an intimate level. Chris is the centre of the attraction, without a doubt, whether it's whirling around singing his famously fragile lines, or hunched over a piano with those notoriously 'Fair Trade' ink-stained hands and fingers. There are gags aplenty, such as "We call this the Michael Bolton tribute section, mainly due to the singer's hair", a self-deprecation that is a part of Chris's personality and will never go away, no matter how massive his band become.

But on this tour – as on the fourth album – there was a sense that this was very much a *band*. Most obviously there was the touring début of the Will Champion-sung 'Death Will Never Conquer', an eye-opener for latecomers to the Coldplay party, as indeed was 'Billie Jean', their oddly compelling (albeit rather bizarre) tribute to the late Michael Jackson. But aside from these specific examples, there was an overall sense of them being a unit. On this tour, Coldplay was a four-man gang, rather than a one-man army.

Then, to the surprise of many fans, only a few months after the fourth album had been shipped to stores, the band announced that they would be releasing a brand new selection of songs on the 'Prospekt's March' EP, to be released in late November 2008. This was a direct result of the highly fertile recording sessions for *Viva La Vida*, with many near-completed songs still available to the band. Guy had already suggested that the recording sessions had been so productive that they almost had another album's worth of material, rather than just enough for an EP.

Usually, if a track isn't included on an album, it's for a good reason. The songs here, however, were very intriguing, definitely displaying a wider palate than on a standard Coldplay album. The opening revisit to 'Life In

Technicolor' saw the album's instrumental opener expanded into a full song with vocals. The lyrics, concerning the end of the world, contrast with the euphoric strings and the fabled track is given a more lavish treatment than on the album, featuring a massive chorus and Jonny's strangely hypnotic guitars. Rather than a 'remix', this feels like a new track and obviously begs the question: why was this song not included on the preceding long player?

Second track, 'Postcards From Far Away', is a 48-second incidental piano piece, a miniature interlude ahead of track three, and decidedly filmic in its flavour. It provides a hint that if Coldplay disband, then Chris could certainly enjoy a career in movie soundtracks.

The more obvious stadium classic, 'Glass Of Water', comes next, with shades of Eno and a monstrous Muse-like guitar riff. The band mix heavyweight 'Politik'-sized substance with a catchy melody to stunning effect and once again one can only ponder why this track, above all, didn't make it on to the album. It's classic Coldplay. Chris, explaining their reasoning, claimed that they were too timid: "[We thought] we'll put out those songs that we were maybe a little shy about putting out."

The band's inclination to experiment in the studio with Eno is evident in the fourth song, 'Rainy Day', which *almost* sees Coldplay do dance. There are even shades of breakbeat, not something you would ever expect to hear from this band. There are also slices of funk in the upbeat canter, which is coloured with lush, staccato strings and quirky changes of rhythm. Eno is absolutely at the fore here, coaxing a jovial yet somehow darkly experimental feel from the song (helped again by an appearance from Davide Rossi's blistering Violectra). Altogether an intriguing number.

Vocal echoes of Radiohead again rear their head on 'Prospekt's March/ Poppyfields', although the more hopeful lyrics contrast with Thom Yorke's sinister linguistic pessimism. The psychedelic guitars of Jonny are once more entrancing. Then Jay-Z pops up – normally a surefire success – but in this context his contribution sounds out of place, disjointed even. In theory this should have been an EP highlight, but it fails to deliver and sounds oddly self-indulgent (by now, an internet 'mash-up' of Coldplay and Jay-Z songs was doing the rounds). The remixed album track 'Lovers In Japan' is more radio-friendly than its album counterpart and was said to have been inspired by the band having played the track better live than in the studio. The EP draws to a close with the fabulous 'Now My Feet Won't Touch The Ground'. The lyrics from 'Life In Technicolor' are reprised as the title of this stripped-down, acoustic track.

It was, above all, an ambitious EP. Far from being designed as a mere schedule-filler, like so many bands' 'unused tracks' projects, this was a clear signal from Coldplay that they were fighting to expand beyond their 'accepted' sound. This was something that Chris himself highlighted when talking to *Rolling Stone*: "We're English so it takes us a while to be really ambitious. [The tracks here] aren't ambitious in a *Kid A* way... but what else are you going to do? Can't keep on trying to make 'Yellow' every day."

Tracks such as 'Glass Of Water' were – in terms of Coldplay at least – much heavier, and this is perhaps why the band ultimately decided against including them on the album. There was an intriguing variety too, not something that the band was famous for. However, unfortunately the critics were lukewarm, with the general consensus being that the better tracks should have been on the album and the weaker tracks were exactly that. "Far more complicated than it needs to be," ridiculed *NME*. "A hefty bout of smoke and mirrors ultimately intended to add some mystery to the Coldplay campaign and reignite interest in *Viva La Vida*... Will it work? Is 'Prospekt's March' a stroke of marketing/brand reigniting/whatever genius? Lord knows." *The Sunday Times* was positive but muted in its praise: "The truth is that these songs are pretty much interchangeable with those on *Viva*. So, if you like that album, this will be a welcome bonus."

This all mattered not, of course, as the EP sold heavily and did indeed reignite interest in both the preceding album and the world tour. Making their way around the world in late 2008, Coldplay received probably the best Christmas present any band could wish for – the news that *Viva La Vida* had been the best-selling album in the world in 2008. Strangely, the UK award season was not kind to Coldplay's world-beating record. Although nominated for 'Best Group', 'Best Live Act', 'Best Single' and 'Best Album', they came away from the Brit Awards ceremony empty-handed. In stark contrast – and a final confirmation if any was needed that the band had genuinely cracked America – the Grammys showered them with three gongs: 'Best Song' and 'Best Record' for 'Viva La Vida', as well as 'Best Album'.

Not being a band content to rest on their laurels, they followed up the EP with a slew of UK arena dates, again taking in the nation's biggest sheds like the O2, the SECC and MEN. These dates took them right through to Christmas, ending in Belfast – and yes, for the London shows, Chris was spotted travelling to the O2 on the Jubilee Line, reading a copy of *The Daily Mirror*. Enticingly, Chris also revealed that he had bought a cheap small keyboard – "one of those you get given for Christmas when you are seven" – and was constantly writing new material on the road. "I write all the time, because it's the only way to make sense of everything."

Yet even during these huge stadium shows in their home country, off the back of the world's biggest-selling album the previous year, the fragility of Chris Martin's persona was on full view. He apologised for not playing more shows in the UK, he said sorry for his hairstyle and numerous other seemingly innocuous things. Talking to *Q* magazine, Will sighed with endearing resignation and offered a reason to be positive: "At the early gigs, he'd say sorry 500 times a night on stage. The year 2000, I think that was the height of the apologies."

CHAPTER 25

A Fresh Start

"Our Wikipedia page says it's due out at the end of the year? Which year?"
Chris Martin commenting in 2009 on web reports
about the next Coldplay album

As the world tour for *Viva...* rumbled along, the band had already started serious work on the next album. Given their previous protracted studio experiences, it was surprising to hear Guy suggest that the new record might even be finished by late 2009. The band spent an initial two weeks in the studio, again with Brian Eno, before heading out to Japan for yet more massive gigs. Almost comically, Brian asked if Chris could stay away from the studio for the first two weeks while the rest of the band got started! Eno's theory was that if the vocalist was not there, then other unusual song ideas might germinate outside of the band's usual structure.

Will was in confident mood: "The first three records were fun to record and tour, and the last record is the start of something new. It's definitely a beginning." Guy told another journalist that the writing process was becoming increasingly varied: "There's no specific way it functions any more, which is really quite exciting, because it means everything is coming from a slightly different place." The band had their 'bakery' studio complex, but there were also rumours that they were holed up in a dilapidated north London church, where they were reported to be "masterminding a brave new direction". At the time of writing, the only snippets about the new material's direction are vague suggestions that it will be "more acoustic". However, one thing is for certain: with Coldplay in the studio, everything is subject to change!

As if catching a mood of change, in December 2009 it was announced that Coldplay were auctioning off much of their studio gear and other memorabilia in an 'End Of Decade Clearout Sale' for charity. This included costumes from the *Viva La Vida* tour, guitars, keyboards, amps, posters, platinum discs "and all sorts of nostalgia". Even the spinning globe featured on the front of *Parachutes* was being sold, as well as Chris and Will's first ever guitars. From December 17 until December 31, the items were listed on the auction site eBay and open to anyone to purchase. Everything was either signed by the four band members or accompanied by a certificate of authenticity, again signed by Coldplay. Proceeds went to Kids Company, which is a charity helping vulnerable children and young people in London.

While Coldplay were busy in the studio, Guy's side project, Apparatjik, released their first album in February 2010. Described as "a music and art project fusing scientific interest and artistic effort and consisting of Guy Berryman, Jonas Bjerre, Magne F and Martin", the idea obviously intrigued millions of Coldplay fans worldwide. Interestingly, the band's name translates as "agent of the apparatus". Elsewhere, Guy's artistic side was also visible when he launched another new project, asking fans to submit photographs. His website post simply said that he was looking for "old photographs, for a personal art project. They can be good photos, or completely out of focus. They can be black and white or colour. The point is that they are pictures dating back to the Sixties and before, that have been thrown away and found again – rather than your own old family photographs." At the time of writing, there has been no further information on this intriguing request. In late November, news broke of Jonny's wedding to long-time girlfriend Chloe-Lee Evans at a small, private ceremony in London. Otherwise, the band has been noticeably quiet publicly, as they are often wont to do when recording new material.

And as if to remind the cynics that the band were still a powerful champion of numerous causes, when Haiti was hit by a devastating earthquake they were quick to respond to calls for help. Having first visited the country back in 2002, Chris still recalled his own experiences. "When something that terrible and tragic happens, you have to play to your strengths, to do anything you can to help," he told the press. "We're useless 'on the ground', as it were. So the best thing we can do is what we do." What they did was assist with a huge telethon organised by actor George Clooney, which raised millions of dollars for the relief fund.

Then, after all the multi-million-selling albums, countless stadium tours, magazine front covers and hyper-celebrity, the band finally, thankfully, *actually* hit the big time – by being invited to appear on an episode of *The Simpsons*. The band had previously been invited backstage some seven years earlier to watch how the programme was made, but at that point they were simply not a big enough draw to be asked to actually appear. Not so now. Their Season 21 appearance in an episode called 'Million Dollar Maybe' saw Homer win a million-dollar lottery and spend his money in various bizarre ways, such as hiring Coldplay to perform for him and Bart. The band are stopped halfway through their set so that Bart can use the toilet and later Homer turns down an offer to join them on stage playing the tambourine. As the band are massive fans of the show, the decision to take part was instant. However, only Chris speaks, the other three being just 'extras'. "We have no voices," said Jonny. "The story of our lives!"

It is unlikely that Chris Martin is going to need adrenalin injections to restart a heart riddled with hard drugs; he probably isn't going to be thrown off a tour due to constant and debilitating alcohol consumption; Iggy, Mötley Crüe, *et al* he is not. But he does not pretend to be anything other than what he is. When Dave Gahan plunged into an abyss of drug use and self-doubt, he later admitted that to a degree he was simply attempting to look – and live – like a rock icon. Grainy pictures of a tattooed Gahan, his straggly locks falling on to his lean but wasted shoulders, holding a crucifix pose in front of 80,000 fans are some of the most 'iconic' and atmospheric images ever captured. But the inspirational Gahan, newly clean and fighting fit, has himself shunned this persona as effectively a fallacy.

Chris Martin has trodden a rather more benign path from the start. Likewise his bandmates. They are, ultimately, just being themselves. Their campaigns for various causes seem – oddly – to annoy as many people as they impress, but it's difficult to chide a man (and indeed a band) who can raise half a million dollars by letting one person sing one song on stage with them.

For all the criticism aimed at his 'worthiness' and well-to-do childhood, there is one accusation that cannot be levelled at Chris Martin: a lack of authenticity. He exists in a rarefied world of super-celebrity and ultra-wealth, but that is not a position he sought out, it is simply a by-product of his creativity. You cannot doubt that he is a frontman who captivates. Yet if he were to write about the mundanity of life, or of a dark childhood of deprivation, he would instantly be lampooned as a fraud. He writes about subjects that he is qualified to write about: life, love and relationships.

The rage that Chris seemed to inexplicably provoke in journalists and public alike in the band's early days seems to have subsided, perhaps thanks in no small part to his much more jovial public demeanour on later album campaigns. Not that in the early days of Coldplay he was dour – far from it, but this was, after all, a very young man who had just been catapulted from student digs into the surreal world of celebrity. It would have taken a very worldly wise pair of shoulders not to feel the strain.

Speaking to *Rolling Stone*, Chris himself said: "We don't see rock 'n' roll as being about coke-taking, leather-trouser-wearing rebellion, because that to us is not rebellion any more. The spirit of rock 'n' roll is *freedom*. It's about following what you believe in and not caring what anyone else says. And if that means writing something on your hand, then you've got to write something on your hand. It doesn't matter if you don't look as cool as The Ramones – you're never going to, anyway. So I know that we'll be ridiculed for this and look stupid for that. But as long as we believe in what we're doing, we can't apologise for it.'

The privacy that the band all closely guard is not unique to them. In the post-millennial world, celebrities are constantly fighting with the press over exactly how much of their 'private' lives should be open to the public. Chris and Gwyneth understand that their ultra-high-profile means they cannot simply pop to the shops without being photographed, but they obviously feel there should be limits.

In this sense, Chris Martin is a very modern rock star. His career is like a Facebook profile – it's a public forum, but one that he wants to set certain limits and parameters on. You can see so much, but beyond that, you have to be one of his 'friends'.

As Chris moves through his thirties, he seems ideally placed to grow older gracefully as a rock star. Perhaps Coldplay's more mellow canon will help Chris maintain his integrity. For his part, he remains unconvinced and has even suggested that he might bow out of the spotlight altogether. Speaking to the *New York Post*, he said, "When I'm 40, too old to be a rock star, I plan to go back to college to study classical music." You wouldn't envy the lecturer who has to tell him that his latest composition doesn't really work.

His band, Coldplay, have sold in excess of 50 million albums. They have unarguably 'cracked' America. But when it is all stripped back, when the awards, chart-topping records, sold-out stadiums and superstar headlines have been and gone, there is at the core of the band an honesty and authenticity that refuses to be twisted by the machinations of the fame game. "Coldplay's struggles and the fact that people did laugh at them made them a lot more level-headed," muses Fierce Panda's Simon Williams. "They were honest, they didn't really help themselves by talking about Genesis in a lot of the early interviews, but rather that than some snotty shite talking about, 'We are the new Sex Pistols'. I always got the impression that Coldplay were nice guys, in an evil world."

And for now at least, it is a world that they do, indeed, rule.